Contents

The Shrew 6	The Zebra 36	The Elephant Seal and the Walrus ... 63	The Chameleon 90
Rats and Mice 7	The Elephant 37	Seals and Sea Lions 64	Lizards 91
The Hedgehog 8	The Hippopotamus . 38		The Komodo Dragon 92
The Porcupine 9	The Wild Boar 39	Dolphins 65	The Sea Turtle 93
The Bat.......... 10	The Chamois 40	The Killer Whale ... 66	Frogs and Toads.... 94
The Mole 11	The Gazelle 41	The Blue Whale.... 67	The Sea Horse 96
The Beaver....... 12	The Bison......... 42	The Swallow 68	The Eel........... 97
The Marmot....... 13	The Musk Ox...... 43	The Toucan 69	The Salmon 98
The Prairie Dog.... 14	The Water-Buffalo.. 44	The Woodpecker ... 70	The Shark 99
The Squirrel....... 15	The Giraffe 45	Owls.............. 71	Strange Fish 100
The Hare 16	The Okapi 46	The Cuckoo 72	The Starfish 102
The Meerkat 17	The Stag 47	Parrots 73	Some Molluscs.... 103
The Cheetah 18	The Camel and the Dromedary... 48	The Seagull 74	More Molluscs.... 104
The Lion 19		The Puffin 75	Some Crustaceans 106
The Tiger 20	The Llama 49	The Penguin....... 76	The Sea Anemone 108
The Leopard 21	The Sloth 50	The Pelican 77	
The Lynx 22	The Giant Anteater . 51	The Eagle 78	The Octopus 109
The Hyena 23	The Pangolin 52	The Vulture 79	The Piranha 110
The Otter 24	The Armadillo 53	The Flamingo 80	The Ladybird..... 111
The Polecat 25	The Duck-billed Platypus... 54	The Heron 81	Ants 112
The Badger 26		The Kiwi 82	Insects 113
The Racoon 27	...and the Spiny Anteater 55	The Ostrich 83	Termites 116
The Giant Panda .. 28		The Swan 84	Wasps 117
The Brown Bear .. 29	Some Marsupials... 56	The Stork 85	Bees 118
The Polar Bear 30	The Kangaroo 57	The Peacock...... 86	Butterflies and Moths 120
The Wolf 31	The Koala Bear 58	Crocodiles and Alligators 87	
The Fox 32	Lemurs........... 59		Spiders 122
The Jackal 33	The Chimpanzee ... 60	Snakes 88	The Scorpion 124
The Rhinoceros 34	The Orang-Utan ... 61		
The Tapir 35	Other Monkeys ... 62		

Published in the UK in 1995 by Schofield & Sims Limited, Huddersfield, England

All rights reserved.
No part of this publication may be reproduced, stored in a retrieval system, or transmitted in any form, or by any means, electronic, mechanical, photocopying, recording or otherwise, without the prior permission of the copyright holders.

0 7217 5028 1

© Éditions Fleurus, Paris

The Animal World

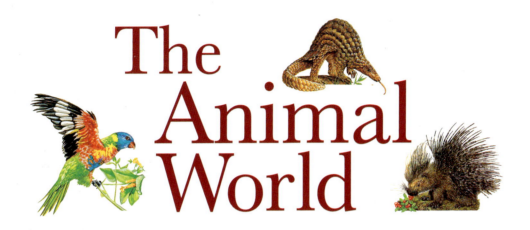

Original text by
Laurence Boukobza
Annick Moulinier

Illustrations by
Danielle Beck
Catherine Loget

Original concept by
Emilie Beaumont

SCHOFIELD & SIMS

The Shrew

The shrew has a pointed snout, tiny eyes and a tail almost as long as its body. It has brown fur with a lighter brown chest. It lives in both flat and hilly country.

Where are shrews found?
Shrews are timid by nature and hide in the grass, under leaves, under the snow or even in tunnels dug by voles.

Even if they cannot be seen, shrews can often be heard, making a noise like fledgling birds. Shrews live alone and only come together to mate.

Eat or die!
A shrew feeds for 3 hours, then rests for 3 hours. If it does not eat after 3 hours, it will die. It is active by both day and night. Shrews eat insects and grasshoppers. They also eat earthworms and slugs.

Do shrews live long?
Shrews live between 6 months and a year. Their dead bodies are often found whole because their strong smell puts other animals off eating them.

At night, shrews are often hunted by owls.

Which is the smallest mammal in the world?
Savi's pigmy shrew: it is 6 cm from nose to tail-tip.

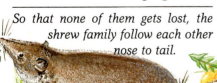

So that none of them gets lost, the shrew family follow each other nose to tail.

Rats and Mice

To catch rats and mice?
Make a din! They hate noise, and would rather risk being killed escaping from noise than remaining near it.

Do rats and mice travel far?
No, they rarely leave their home territory because they know that they can easily get food nearby.

1 + 1 = 20 million!
A female rat can be pregnant up to 7 times a year. She gives birth to between 6 and 12 babies at a time. Three months later, these baby rats will be ready to breed. In 3 years, a pair of rats could have 20 million descendants!

There are lots of different rats and mice, but the best known are the brown rat and the field mouse. Brown rats often live in packs in sewers. They are excellent swimmers. Field mice live in fields, woods and gardens.

Do rats eat a lot?
Rats eat anything! Plastic-coated wires, wood, leather, anything out of dustbins – they eat them all. They destroy crops and can often cause havoc by gnawing through electric cables.

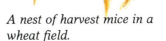

A nest of harvest mice in a wheat field.

The muskrat lives in the streams and lakes of North America. ▶

The Hedgehog

When the hedgehog starts to move around the forest, we know that spring is coming. In winter, it rolls up into a ball and sleeps without needing to eat. In spring, it wakes up. At night, it travels about with its ears alert and its snout in the earth, searching for food.

What does the hedgehog do when frightened?

If something frightens or disturbs the hedgehog, it puts its head between its feet and rolls into a ball. This puts a wall of sharp prickles between the animal and its enemy.

A hedgehog's prickles are made up of small clumps of bristles.

What do hedgehogs eat?

Hedgehogs eat snails, slugs, insects, mice and rats. A hedgehog will even attack a poisonous snake. It is not affected by snake bites. Once the snake is dead, the hedgehog happily eats it. A hedgehog spends half its life hunting.

What are young hedgehogs like?

They are born blind and naked. After several hours, soft, white, prickles start to appear. Their spines quickly become brown and hard like those of their parents.

Baby hedgehogs cannot roll themselves into a ball until they are much older.

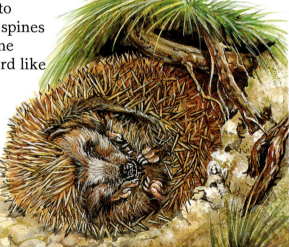

The Porcupine

What does it do during the day?
The porcupine spends the day in the deep burrow it has dug out. It comes out at night to hunt for food.

How does it attract a mate?
A male porcupine preens himself, then struts about in front of the female. If she takes no notice of him, the male runs up to her and rattles his quills. Mating takes place at night. Baby porcupines have soft fur, not quills, when they are born.

The porcupine has a body covered in pointed spines or quills. Although it looks like a hedgehog, the two animals are not related. The porcupine is one of the biggest rodents. It eats fruit, grass, roots and tree bark, which it tears with its strong claws.

Is the porcupine aggressive?
When angry, it is a formidable sight. It charges backwards at its enemy with its quills erect. Many animals retreat when they see a porcupine.

The Bat

Strangely enough, the bat is a mammal. It has 2 long wings and is the only mammal capable of flying like a bird. Bats come out at twilight to hunt, and return to their shelter at dawn, squeaking loudly before going to sleep.

Why upside down?
Bats hang upside down to groom themselves, to sleep, to hibernate, and to give birth. During the day, they roost head downwards in caves, old barns or tall trees.

How do bats navigate?
By a kind of radar. The bat sends out an ultrasonic signal which reflects back an echo when it touches an object. The time taken for the echo to return allows the bat to locate the object.

Are all bats the same?
No. There are many types of bats and they do not all have the same diet. Some of them eat insects, some prefer fruit or fish, and others, such as the vampire bat which lives in Central and South America, drink the blood of animals – and sometimes even of people!

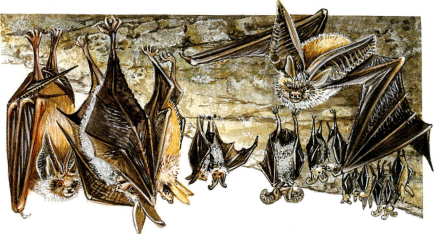

Many bats hibernate in winter, when insects become scarce. During this time, their temperature drops and they hang clustered together to keep warm.

The Mole

The mole lives in the earth underneath fields and gardens. It is a hungry little creature and spends most of its time digging out tunnels whilst searching for something to eat. It eats worms, grubs – and sometimes even other moles! It has sharp, pointed teeth that help it to chew through anything hard.

Is the mole really blind?
Almost. It has two tiny eyes no larger than pinpricks and can only just distinguish between day and night. However, its ears and nose are extremely sensitive.

How does it dig out its tunnels?
It uses its pointed snout and front paws. These strong paws look almost like human hands, and are used in a breast-stroke action. The mole burrows through the earth with its snout, and then uses its spade-like paws to push the earth behind it. When there is too much earth in the tunnel, the mole digs upwards and pushes out the earth to make the mounds we call molehills.

What do baby moles look like?
They are born completely naked and their velvety fur doesn't start to grow until they are about 15 days old. During this time, they remain in the cosy, warm nest, where their mother suckles them for over a month.

The mole's pointed muzzle and hidden mouth prevent it from swallowing earth.

The mole gives birth to 4 or 5 young at a time.

The Beaver

Using its tail and hind legs to balance, the beaver grasps the tree-trunk between its front paws and leans its head to one side to attack the wood with its long, sharp front teeth. It gnaws around the trunk and, when the tree has fallen, nibbles it up into smaller branches. It likes to gnaw willow, poplar, alder, elm and oak trees.

Cross-section of a beaver's lodge (below): it looks like a rounded heap of branches. Usually, there is one main chamber above the level of the water and an entrance underneath the water, deeper than one metre so that it does not get blocked by ice.

The beaver is a rodent which always lives near trees and water. It builds dams, sometimes more than 4 metres high, in which it constructs its living quarters, called a lodge. Beavers can live for about 20 years.

Why a dam?
By building a dam, the beaver creates an artificial lake where the water is deep and will not freeze completely. It is here that the animal builds its lodge. The dam is built of twigs and branches woven together and made stronger with mud and leaves. It is so watertight that on many rivers the water stops flowing altogether. The lodges are built in the same way as the dams. The beaver hoards its food for winter in the lodge. Its main food is the bark and shoots of the trees it gnaws.

Is the beaver's tail useful?
Very! It is wide and flat and acts as a rudder when the animal swims, and as a support on the ground when it is gnawing. Also, when an enemy approaches, the beaver splashes its tail up and down in the water. This sound acts as a warning signal for the beavers in other lodges.

The Marmot

The female marmot keeps a watchful eye on her little ones.

The marmot is a small, short-legged rodent with pointed teeth, powerful claws and thick brown fur. It lives in the mountains in the summer, in family groups of between 4 and 15 animals. Marmots eat large amounts of food during the summer and become very fat. This prepares them for the long winter hibernation during which a marmot may lose a quarter of its weight.

How do they survive the winter?
At the end of September, the marmots come down into the fields and start to dig their burrows. Here, deep underground inside a large chamber, they all settle down together on a nest of hay and spend the winter fast asleep.

Watch out – there's a stranger about!
When a marmot doesn't recognise another marmot's smell, it usually chases it away. However, if an enemy is nearby, the unknown marmot will be allowed into the burrow until danger is past.

Who's on guard in case of danger?
Marmots always have a sentry on guard. This marmot stands on its hind legs and keeps watch whilst the others play or feed. If danger threatens, the guard whistles very loudly and all the other marmots run to hide in the burrow.

The Prairie Dog

This little American rodent doesn't look like a dog at all, but it makes a noise like barking and that's where its name comes from. The animal is actually a type of squirrel.

Do prairie dogs live in kennels?
Of course not! They dig out huge burrows, called towns, where each family has its own den. Most burrows have mounds of earth at the entrance to keep water out and to provide a lookout post. Some 'towns' may consist of several thousand individuals and cover several square kilometres.

When danger threatens?
One prairie dog guards the entrance of each burrow whilst the others feed or play or have a nap in the sun. If an enemy appears, the 'guard dog' gets on its hind legs and barks to warn the others.

Where does it keep its food?
The prairie dog doesn't keep a stock of food. Everything it eats – nuts, fruits, leaves and insects – it has to leave its burrow to find. The prairie dog likes to eat outside in the sunshine. And if it's raining or cold, the animal remains in its den without eating or drinking. But it won't die of hunger because it has abundant reserves of fat.

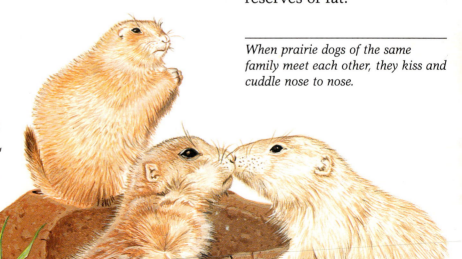

When prairie dogs of the same family meet each other, they kiss and cuddle nose to nose.

The Squirrel

The squirrel is a small rodent with grey or red fur. Its beautiful, feathery tail is almost as long as its body and never stops moving. Always on the alert and in a hurry, the squirrel rushes up tree-trunks or jumps from branch to branch. It has sharp eyes and ears and runs away at the slightest sound.

The squirrel holds the nut with its front paws and breaks the shell with its teeth.

Is its tail useful?
Very useful! It shelters the squirrel from sun and rain and helps it to keep its balance when walking along a thin branch or jumping from one branch to another. It also acts as a parachute if the squirrel has to jump from a tree to escape from danger.

A secret food store?
In autumn, the squirrel gathers its food which consists mainly of nuts and seeds for winter. It buries this 20 or 30 centimetres below the ground, in secret hiding-places which it finds again by using its keen sense of smell. If it forgets where some of them are, all the better: they will grow into new trees!

Do a squirrel's teeth ever stop growing?
No, never. That's because squirrels gnaw endlessly – nuts, tree bark, pine cones, fruit, acorns and buds.

Baby squirrels are born in a nest made of twigs and leaves, called a drey. Sometimes the female squirrel builds her drey out of a deserted magpie nest.

The Hare

The hare is the cousin of the rabbit, but don't confuse them. The hare's ears are longer and its large hind legs make it a very fast animal – especially in a chase. It hides away during the day and only comes out at night to feed on grasses and other plants.

Is the hare a cautious animal?
Very! It never goes back to its resting-place by a direct route. Instead, it runs backwards and forwards and jumps up and down – sometimes as high as one metre. In this way, it can see above the grass and keep watch for its enemies. A hunter and his dog could well be nearby!

Does it live in a burrow?
No, it doesn't. It uses its front paws to scrape out a small dent in the earth, just big enough to lie down in. Or it just lies on the grass. A hare's resting place is called a form. With its ears lying parallel and pointing backwards, the animal is ready to run at the slightest danger. The baby hares, called leverets, are born in the form.

Do hares have boxing matches?
Yes, they do. The males often fight over a female during the mating season. They stand up on their hind legs, face to face, and scratch each other, pulling out tufts of fur.

The hare family – a doe and her leverets.

The Meerkat

The meerkat, a small, slender creature with a sweet face and a sociable nature, is a relative of the mongoose. Meerkats live in burrows in the deserts of Africa and feed on small rodents, snakes and insects. Their well-developed sense of smell means they can sniff out larvae buried beneath the ground.

Disappearing ears!
Meerkats can close their ears like eyelids. This means that when they are digging their tunnels under the desert, not a single grain of sand gets inside their ears.

The mother meerkat gives her babies lots of affection.

Standing on their hind legs, meerkats look like tiny people.

What is the meerkats' golden rule?
Love and sharing. Always united, never fighting. Meerkats spend lots of time hugging each other, and the adults share out the food amongst the baby meerkats before thinking of themselves.

Meerkats are not at all frightened of snakes or scorpions.

Are meerkats well organised?
Yes, they are experts at organisation. When it is time to hunt, one meerkat looks after the young ones whilst another jumps on to a high branch and carefully surveys the horizon. If an eagle or a jackal appears, the lookout's cries alert the hunters and all the meerkats disappear into their burrows.

The Cheetah

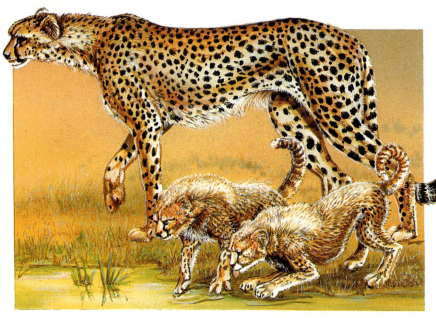

Cheetah cubs are born with a long mane along their neck and back.

The cheetah is easily recognised – it has a slim body with dark spots, a long tail, a small head and long, slender legs. The black 'tear marks' from the corner of each eye make it look as though it is crying. Most cheetahs live in Africa.

Cheetahs hunt gazelles, antelopes and monkeys.

Do they live as a family?
Cheetahs may live in pairs or in a family group, which is led by the strongest male. He decides where the group will go, and chooses which prey to attack and even which female to mate with. Females give birth to 2 or 3 cubs.

Is the cheetah athletic?
Very – its slim, supple body and long legs are perfect for running. The cheetah is the swiftest mammal in the world over a short distance, reaching speeds of 110km/h. But it tires very quickly and has to rest after each chase. For this reason, cheetahs often steal the prey of other animals instead of hunting.

What is unusual about a cheetah's claws?
Unlike other cats, a cheetah cannot sheathe its claws. They dig into the ground and so help the animal to run faster. At the back of each front paw, the cheetah has a very sharp claw called a dew-claw, which it uses to pull down its prey.

How does the cheetah kill its prey?
It stalks its prey from a great distance, then rushes towards it at great speed and pounces. The cheetah kills its prey by biting through its neck.

The Lion

The lion's thunderous roars can be heard from a long way away.

The majestic lion is known as the 'king of beasts'. Most lions live in Africa, in family groups called prides. A lioness gives birth to 2 or 3 cubs at a time and cares for them until they are old enough to hunt for themselves.

Who does the hunting?
The females, sometimes helped by the males. They hunt at dusk or at night and usually kill only to eat. After the prey is killed, the strongest male in the troop eats first and the others wait their turn. The females and cubs eat last.

What does a lion eat?
Mainly zebras, antelopes and other grazing animals. Sometimes lions will eat animal carcasses.

How do lions attack their prey?
Keeping their bodies low, they creep slowly through the tall grass towards their prey. Then the lion jumps on the prey and drags it to the ground, biting into its neck to kill it. In a group, several lions may circle round the prey and drive it towards an ambush hiding in the grass.

Why are lion cubs often in danger?
Playful and curious, the cubs are easy prey on the savannah and many die. Also, when a young male becomes leader he will often kill the cubs of old male lions. So a lioness keeps moving her cubs from one place to another for safety.

The lioness teaches the cubs to hunt.

The Tiger

A tiger's stripes help it to blend in with its surroundings.

This powerful animal lives in Asia, especially India, and likes to hunt alone. Because of its stripes, a tiger is easily camouflaged and is able to surprise its prey. Tigers have very good eyesight and hearing.

What does a tiger eat?
The tiger is a meat-eater and its favourite meal is a deer or a wild boar. It also likes porcupines, despite the prickles, but it will eat monkeys, snakes, frogs, turtles and termites. It can also catch fish. If a tiger is old or ill, it may attack people.

Does the female have many cubs?
No, she doesn't. It takes her two years to raise a family of 2 or 3 cubs. Half the young tigers will die before they reach maturity.

What is the tiger's favourite pastime?
Tigers do not like the heat, so they love to lie in water when they are too hot. They are excellent swimmers.

What else do tigers do?
They must constantly mark out their territory to show where the boundaries are and keep other tigers away. They do this by urinating or leaving droppings. A tiger spends the day resting and comes out at dusk to hunt.

The Leopard

The leopard is a fierce but beautiful big cat that lives in Africa and Asia. It spends its life either hidden in undergrowth or stretched out along the branch of a tree. It may seem to be asleep, but passing prey should beware! It can attack swiftly and kill with one bite. It is a cunning and patient hunter, and can run, jump, climb trees and swim.

Is the leopard a powerful animal?
Extremely! Its strength is legendary and its claws and teeth are formidable. The leopard jumps on its prey and kills it, then drags it away to eat in peace. Leopards have been known to drag prey heavier than themselves high up into a tree to eat.

Is the leopardess a good mother?
Yes, she is. She suckles her cubs and grooms them with long licks. She watches over them very closely and teaches them all the tricks of hunting. At the age of 2, the young leopards leave their mother and have to survive on their own.

What animals are a leopard's prey?
A leopard attacks all living creatures, from rats to gazelles and from zebras to porcupines. It has such good eyesight that it can see as well at night as during the day. It generally hunts at dusk.

The black panther is a type of leopard that lives in forests.

The Lynx

Within its territory, a lynx develops certain habits. It always goes to the same places and has special places for resting and sleeping. With its large, furry paws, a lynx can move easily over snow and ice.

The lynx is a powerful wild cat that lives in Europe, Africa, Asia and America. It has pointed ears with distinctive tufts on the end, and a short tail. The lynx is not as large as other big cats.

Is the lynx a fierce animal?

When faced with an enemy, the lynx can look quite frightening. It screeches, spits, claws at the ground and raises its hackles – surely enough to scare off an attacker!

What does it like to eat?

The lynx is a meat-eater and is very fond of rabbits, hares, squirrels, snakes and birds. It also likes birds' eggs – it is an agile climber. Sometimes, when driven by hunger, the lynx will attack larger animals such as deer, sheep and goats. After a meal, the lynx goes to its lair to rest.

Is the lynx a good hunter?

Yes, the lynx is an excellent hunter and its attack is swift. Although it hunts by night, its sharp eyes and keen hearing allow it to detect its prey easily. Then it creeps up silently and takes its prey by surprise by jumping on its back. It kills by biting its prey through the neck.

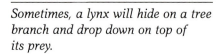

Sometimes, a lynx will hide on a tree branch and drop down on top of its prey.

The Hyena

What does it eat?
Prey it has either caught itself or stolen from other animals. Its stomach digests everything: insects, bones, even other animals' droppings!

Is the hyena really laughing?
No, but when it gets excited near its prey it makes a noise that sounds like laughter.

The mother hyena changes her lair often to protect her young from predators.

Hyenas can be spotted or striped and are found in Africa and Asia. They live in packs and defend their territory well. When the young, 3 at most, are born, they are brown all over, without any markings, their eyes are open and their sharp teeth are already in place.

Are other animals afraid of the hyena?
Yes – it is an excellent hunter and can run quickly for a considerable distance. The hyena has the most powerful jaws of any predator and can crush bones and horns. Hyenas are also crafty thieves and are not afraid of lions or cheetahs.

The Otter

How do otters spend their day?

Both common otters and sea otters spend a lot of time fishing, and even fish at night. In between fishing, they play, sleep or carefully groom themselves. Grooming is particularly important for the sea otter, whose thick brown fur protects it from the cold water.

There are two types of otter: common otters that live in fresh water, and sea otters that live in the sea, though rarely more than a mile from shore. Otters have thick, dense fur and are perfectly adapted to life in the water.

Where does the sea otter find its bedclothes?

It lives in the North Pacific Ocean, where it often sleeps wrapped up amongst the seaweed. This prevents the otter from drifting too far from the shore whilst asleep.

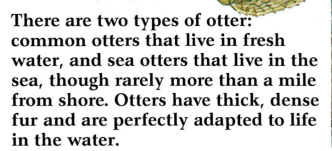

The female otter paddles about with her baby on her stomach.

Do otters like their food?

Very much. They eat fish, crustaceans, frogs and other small creatures. Sea otters also eat octopuses, sea urchins and squid. Otters are intelligent animals and often smash open hard shells with a stone held in their nimble, webbed paws. They float on their backs, using their chests as a table-top!

The Polecat

The polecat has a long body, short legs and a short, furry tail. Although its sharp, bright eyes make it look innocent, don't be deceived. Inside its burrow, the polecat is just waiting for nightfall so that it can go hunting.

Why does the polecat build up stores?
When it has killed its prey, the polecat drags it home. These animals become its food store. When the polecat gets hungry, it can have a tasty snack! All kinds of creatures are found in a polecat's burrow.

What do polecats eat?
The polecat is a carnivore. It eats small rodents, fish, birds and even snakes. It also catches fish. If a polecat lives in the country, it will visit farms and kill rabbits and poultry. It kills its prey by biting through its neck. Sometimes polecats play together, trying to trap each other by the skin of the neck as if they are prey.

Where do polecats live?
Almost everywhere: in the country, in the mountains, or on the coast. They live in trees, rabbit holes, among rocks, or under piles of wood.

How does the polecat defend itself?
It turns around, lifts up its tail and sprays out a nasty-smelling liquid from glands near its bottom. This is enough to deter most attackers.

The Badger

The badger is about as large as a medium-sized dog. It lives in a burrow known as a sett, which it digs out by using the powerful claws on its front legs. Badgers come out at night to hunt. Their keen sense of smell helps them to find food. When a badger catches its prey, it holds it between its teeth and shakes it to death.

Is the badger houseproud?
Yes, very. Inside the sett, the badger makes a nest of grasses and dead leaves, where it sleeps and rears its young. It does not allow any rubbish in its sett, so it cleans out its living quarters regularly and never brings food inside. Badgers eat worms, mice, moles and other small creatures. They also love honey.

What about a toilet?
When it comes to cleanliness, the badger thinks of everything! Above the ground around its territory, it digs out special holes to use as toilets.

How does a badger chase away intruders?
Faced with something it doesn't like, all the bristles on a badger's back stand up and it grunts fiercely to frighten away the intruder. But if it meets a badger it knows, they greet each other by rubbing their bottoms together.

What do badgers do in winter?
Badgers do not truly hibernate because their body temperature does not drop in winter. They stay below ground only if the weather is really bad.

Why is the badger doing a handstand?
It isn't. It has glands under its tail, and by rubbing its rear end against a tree-trunk the badger leaves its scent behind to mark the boundary of its territory.

The Racoon

The racoon often lives near a river, where there is a plentiful supply of food.

Are racoons very active?
Yes, they are excellent swimmers and champion tree climbers. Their front paws have long claws which help them to cling to tree-trunks. That's very useful because they steal birds' eggs, too!

Should people be afraid of racoons?
Racoons can get rabies, which is a disease spread through bites. Racoons are greedy animals and sometimes live in barns and haylofts near to humans. So there is a risk of catching rabies.

The racoon looks very mischievous, with its bright eyes peeping through the highwayman's mask across its face. In America, where it lives, the racoon is always looking for food, and regularly goes into towns to raid people's dustbins.

Where do racoons find their food?
Not always in the dustbin! They also spend a lot of time in the water. They rummage among the stones in the river bed with their paws to catch crayfish, frogs and shellfish. They also eat nuts, fruit, seeds, corn and small animals.

Racoons live in trees or in dens on the ground. The female racoon raises her young in a hollow tree stump.

The Giant Panda

A baby panda cannot walk until it is 4 months old, so its mother carries it everywhere.

The giant panda is like a large white bear with black arms and legs, round black ears, black eyes, and a thick coat that protects it from the cold. It lives a solitary life in the mountains of China, except during the mating season when the male and female meet.

What do pandas eat?
Twenty million years ago pandas were meat-eaters, but now they eat mainly bamboo, which they do not digest very well. They also eat insects, fish, eggs, berries and wild flowers. They spend 14 hours a day eating, to make sure that they get enough nourishment from their food.

Is the baby panda also a giant?
No, it's tiny when born – not much bigger than a kitten. It's blind and is covered in sparse white hair. By the end of a month, it has its distinctive panda markings. The female panda can look after only one cub at a time. If she has twins, one usually dies.

Are there many pandas in the world?
No, they are an endangered species – there are only about 1000 left in the wild. This is because the bamboo forests are being cut down, so there is not enough for the pandas to feed on and they frequently starve to death.

Panda cubs are very playful and love doing somersaults!

The Brown Bear

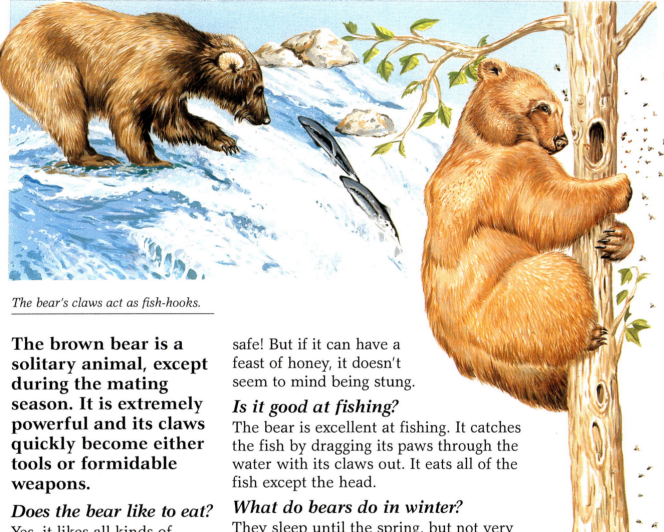

The bear's claws act as fish-hooks.

The brown bear is a solitary animal, except during the mating season. It is extremely powerful and its claws quickly become either tools or formidable weapons.

Does the bear like to eat?
Yes, it likes all kinds of things – insects, berries, rodents, fish, fruit, crops. Such an animal is called an omnivore.

What is the bear's favourite food?
Honey. The bear's thick fur protects it from bee stings, though its snout is not as safe! But if it can have a feast of honey, it doesn't seem to mind being stung.

Is it good at fishing?
The bear is excellent at fishing. It catches the fish by dragging its paws through the water with its claws out. It eats all of the fish except the head.

What do bears do in winter?
They sleep until the spring, but not very deeply. The female gives birth in her lair or in the base of a tree. The cubs grow snuggled up to their mother until the month of March, when they emerge into the world.

The Polar Bear

What is its favourite food?
The polar bear mostly attacks seals, but it will also eat dead whales, small animals, birds and berries. It finds food with the help of its keen sense of smell, which allows it to locate a dead whale far underneath the surface of the ocean. It can stay under the water and ice for more than 2 minutes.

As soon as a seal comes to the surface to breathe, the polar bear catches and eats it.

The polar bear is the largest carnivorous land animal. This powerful animal lives in very cold areas, but its thick fur keeps it warm. It spends much of its time in the water where it swims effortlessly, often like a dog – paddling with its front legs. On land it can run very quickly.

Polar bear cubs play all day long.

Where does the female spend the winter?
In a hole which she scoops out of the snow. There, sheltered from the cold, she gives birth to her young and stays in her den with them until the spring. During this time, the babies suckle but the mother does not eat anything.

The polar bear is as fast in the water as on land.

The Wolf

Wolves communicate with each other by howling.

Wolves usually live in packs, controlled and guided by a dominant male and female. Old wolves who have been rejected by the pack live alone, but never far away from the others. Wolf cubs are raised in a lair and are suckled for about a month. The father stays with the family until the cubs are grown. If anything happens to the mother, he takes care of the cubs.

How do wolves mark their territory?
They urinate and scratch the earth around their lair and also scratch certain landmarks in their territory, such as trees. Wolves have a highly-developed sense of smell, so these smells and marks define their borders. Sometimes they also howl, as if to say to others "This is my home here!"

The wolf digs out hiding-places. What are these for?
These hiding-places are the wolf's pantry. The male stores meat for the female whilst she is busy raising the cubs. Then, when she is hungry, she can find these stores. When one of the stores becomes empty, the wolf urinates on it to remind himself where it is.

When wolves fight, do they stay angry for long?
No. Blood is rarely drawn in a fight between wolves of the same pack. When a wolf loses a fight, it rolls over on its back, lays its ears flat and offers its throat to the winner. It is saying "I've lost – you're the boss."

The Fox

The vixen is a wonderful mother and protects her cubs fiercely from any danger.

A pointed muzzle and ears, a beautiful bushy tail, narrow eyes and a crafty smile – that's the fox. It lives in a burrow, or earth, which it has either dug out itself or stolen from another creature. The fox is alert and agile – it jumps and swims well.

Who are the fox's enemies?
People, mainly. The fox is often hunted in the countryside, where it is considered to be a pest. Some types of fox are also hunted for their fur.

What does it eat?
The fox seizes every opportunity to feed itself. It eats everything – earthworms, which it pulls from the soil without breaking them, mice, rabbits, beetles, fruits, birds, fish and carrion. In towns, where it can now be seen regularly, it will often eat the contents of people's dustbins!

How do foxes hunt?
Sometimes a fox will creep up on its prey, and sometimes it will stalk its victim or lie in wait for it. Its sight, hearing and sense of smell are excellent. Generally, foxes lie low during the day and only come out to hunt at night.

The Arctic fox has shorter ears than other foxes. In winter, its fur becomes white. It can survive in very low temperatures.

The fox buries its prey to save it for later.

The Jackal

The jackal looks like a thin dog: it has a pointed muzzle, large ears and a bushy tail. Its long, muscular legs help it to run quickly. Jackals usually live on their own or in small family groups. Couples live together for a long time and have many offspring. When raising their cubs, they may be assisted by other jackals, called 'helpers'.

What is a helper?
In many families, young jackals about a year old decide to stay with their parents. This is very useful because they feed and look after their younger brothers and sisters. Thanks to them, more baby jackals reach adulthood.

Is family life important?
Very. A family of jackals is made up of father, mother, cubs and helpers. Jackals greet each other by wagging their tails and touching noses – just like dogs. Often the male and female hunt in pairs. They become aggressive in front of a jackal of the same sex.

What do jackals eat?
Whatever they can find – rodents, insects, frogs, fruit, lizards, birds, small animals. They also eat carrion sometimes. Jackals hide stores of food, as foxes do.

What do the cubs eat?
At first, they suckle from their mother. As they get older, the parents and helpers regurgitate food for them.

The Rhinoceros

The rhinoceros is a large, powerful animal. Rhinos are short sighted and the black rhinoceros, in particular, has a bad temper. It reacts quickly to strange smells and noises – it charges straight towards them! The white rhino is not quite so aggressive. The rhino is a herbivore – it eats grass and plants.

The rhinoceros is often accompanied by small birds called 'tick-birds' which pick the irritating insects off its skin.

Why does the rhinoceros roll in the mud?
Despite its thick skin, the animal is very sensitive to insect bites. To get rid of the insects, the rhino takes a mud bath. When the mud dries, it forms a crust that helps to protect the animal's skin.

What does the rhino do each evening?
It goes in search of food, and is also on the look-out for a mud bath.

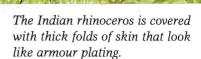

The Indian rhinoceros is covered with thick folds of skin that look like armour plating.

Are there many rhinos left?
No. They are threatened with extinction and are strictly protected. But poachers still kill them to sell their horns.

The 'white' rhinoceros gets its name from its 'wide' mouth.

The Tapir

The size of a large pig, the tapir is a solitary animal except in the mating season. It sleeps during the day and wakes up at night, when it bathes and goes in search of food. Tapirs are very greedy and eat an enormous amount of fruit. They also like lichen and moss.

The baby tapir is born with rows of white spots, like a wild boar. These provide excellent camouflage, but gradually disappear.

The Malayan tapir looks as though it is wearing a white blanket! It lives in South-East Asia.

Is the tapir threatened?
The tapir is very threatened – its thick skin makes excellent leather. In the mating season, the male tapir gives a piercing whistle and the female replies in the same way. People imitate this whistle and the unsuspecting tapir is captured.

Does it defend itself if attacked?
Only very rarely does the tapir defend itself. Usually, it runs away to find some water where it can hide. It loves water and is an excellent swimmer – it can cover several dozen metres in a dive before coming up for air. It often has a mud bath to get rid of parasites.

The Zebra

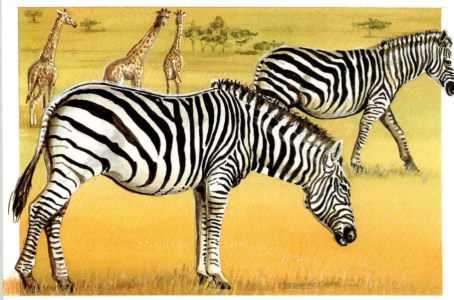

Zebras are never far from giraffes.

Are zebras born with stripes?
Yes, even in its mother's womb a baby zebra is striped. But when it is young its stripes are light coloured. They become darker with age. Although they look similar, each zebra's stripes are different. Their black and white pyjamas are perfect camouflage for the time of day when the lion begins hunting – nightfall.

Are zebras alert?
Very – even the babies are smart. As soon as they are

The African savannah is home to many herds of zebra. These beautifully striped animals

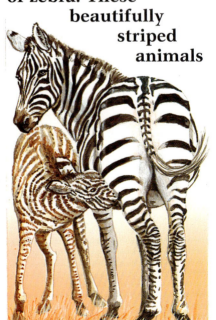

At night, a zebra's stripes help it to become almost invisible.

often graze amongst giraffes and antelopes. Like antelopes, zebras can run very quickly – which is just as well, since they are often pursued by lions and other big cats.

born they stand up, so that they can run away from the slightest danger – before being fed if necessary! During the day, zebras stay near giraffes, who, being so tall, can see far away and give early warning of danger.

The Elephant

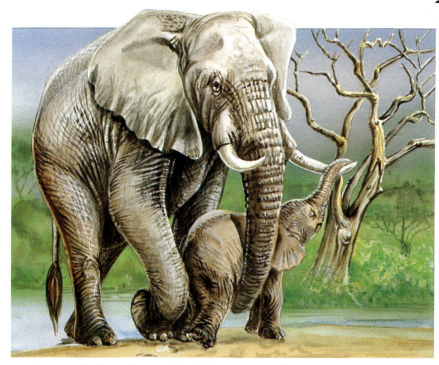
The largest elephants live on the African savannah.

The elephant is the largest land mammal. It can be 4 metres tall and can weigh as much as 100 people. It is very strong, but does not like fighting. Elephants live in a herd with an old female as leader. They are constantly on the move always looking for vegetation to eat and water to drink.

Is the elephant calf well cared for?
Oh yes! The mother pays a lot of attention to her baby. She feeds it with her rich, sweet milk, and helps it to walk with the herd. It holds on to its mother's tail with its trunk.

What's the trunk used for?
An elephant does everything with its trunk. It uses it for drinking, smelling, picking leaves, having a dust-bath or a shower, and for communicating with other elephants.

An elephant's tusks can be over 3 metres long.

Indian elephants have smaller ears.

When an elephant is angry, it waggles its ears and charges at whatever is annoying it, with its trunk stretched out in front.

The Hippopotamus

What a big, lazy creature the hippopotamus is! It spends all day wallowing in shallow water and mud. It is more at home in water than on land.

Where is the baby hippopotamus born?
In the water. The mother helps it to reach the surface so that it can breathe. She teaches it to swim and feeds it for almost a year. When she moves about, she carries the baby on her back to protect it from crocodiles.

The baby hippo feeds under water.

Does the hippopotamus sleep at night?
No, it comes out of the water to nibble the leaves and grass which it loves. Sometimes it has to travel a very long way to find food, but if the hippo is hungry it doesn't mind the journey.

What does it stay in the water for?
The hippopotamus does not like the heat and its skin dries up very quickly. Also, it is often attacked by a nasty insect that stings the

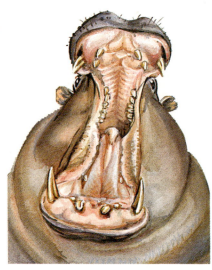

The hippopotamus has a huge mouth with enormous curved teeth like tusks.

hippo's eyelids and sucks its blood. To escape, the hippo dives under water.

Why does the male hippopotamus yawn?
He isn't yawning. What he's doing is showing off how strong he is to another male by opening his mouth wide and growling.

The Wild Boar

A sow and her piglets – they will lose their stripes as they get older.

The wild boar is a type of pig. It has short, thin legs, a long snout, and a body that is covered with strong hairs called bristles. Its tusks are for fighting and also for foraging in the earth for food. Wild boars are sociable creatures and live in the forest in herds consisting of females and young, led by an old sow. The males live alone, briefly joining the herd in winter for the mating season.

How does it clean itself?
The wild boar's bristles are often infested with fleas and mites. To get rid of them, it needs a mud-bath and a good rub up against a tree.

A big family?
A sow may have 10 to 14 piglets at a time. She is a good mother who raises her babies well and defends them courageously.

What a snout – is it useful?
Very. The wild boar uses its snout to sniff out food, even underground. It eats root vegetables, fruit, nuts, worms, reptiles, mice, and birds, with a little soil to help the digestion.

Where do they live?
During the day, wild boars rest in a quiet part of the wood or forest, in a shelter made of thin twigs, dry grass and dead leaves.

Let's get rid of those fleas!

The Chamois

The chamois is light and quick on its feet.

The chamois is a type of deer that lives in the mountains of Europe. Its hide is very tough and its hair is short in summer, but grows long and thick in winter to protect it from the cold. Its coat also changes colour, turning from dark grey in autumn to light brown in spring. The chamois does not like hot weather.

Why does the chamois jump?
Usually, a chamois steps daintily over the rocks. When it jumps, it means it is alert and watchful. The chamois is always on guard.

In autumn, the chamois leaves the mountain and spends winter in the forest below. Here, it will be easier for it to find food. It eats buds, wild fruit and grasses.

Is it a nervous animal?
Living as it does in the peace of the mountains, the slightest noise or unusual smell makes it nervous and uneasy. The chamois is very agile and is an excellent climber.

How old is a chamois?
To tell the age of a chamois, count the number of rings on its horns. It has one ring per year.

Why does it lick snow?
A chamois does not drink much. When the animal is thirsty, it licks snow. This is how it gets the water it needs.

The Gazelle

Males will fight for a female or for a territory.

The gazelle is one of the most graceful animals of Africa and Asia. It is a type of small antelope that lives in packs. Each pack has its own territory. The gazelle eats leaves and grass, which it ruminates. This means that it swallows its food but does not digest it straight away. Instead, it brings the food back into its mouth later as pellets, which it then chews slowly before swallowing and finally digesting.

Do gazelles stay in the same place?

No, they travel long distances to find food and water, and are always on the move.

How does the gazelle protect itself from its enemies?

The gazelle has a white band along its body. This helps to camouflage the animal. Also, it has excellent hearing and eyesight, and a keen sense of smell. It can spot an enemy a long way away and make a rapid escape. Some gazelles can run at over 70 km/h.

But baby gazelles are easy prey for lions, baboons and eagles.

Do male gazelles have a separate territory?

Yes, and this is very important. The females are not interested in a male unless he has his own territory, and they refuse to mate with a male who does not possess one.

The gazelle stands on its hind legs to look for the tastiest leaves at the tops of the trees.

The Bison

The bison is the largest mammal in North America. It can weigh over a tonne. It is an amazing animal to look at, with the mane and tail of a lion, the hump of a camel, and the horns and strength of a bull.

Does the bison feel the cold?
Because of its thick fur, the bison doesn't feel the cold. In winter, when snow falls during the night, it can cover the animal completely. In the morning – no problem: with a quick shake, the bison gets rid of its white blanket. When it is hungry, the animal uses its muzzle to dig beneath the snow for grass.

For a long time, bison were hunted for their skins and for meat. Now they live in reserves where they are protected. They travel about in herds and when they smell danger they run away, running closely together and led by a huge male.

Does it have trouble seeing?
Yes, the bison is very short-sighted, but fortunately its hearing and sense of smell are excellent. Thanks to these, the bison can detect the tiniest source of water from many kilometres away.

What is the bison's favourite game?
The dirtier the bison is, the happier it is. It loves to wallow and roll in mud. The mud then dries on the bison's fur and is an excellent cure for the insects that are always tickling the animal.

The Musk Ox

Why do the animals stand in a circle?
To defend themselves against their enemies. The females and young ones stand in the centre so that they are not attacked. The adult males surround them to give them as much protection as possible.

Does the musk ox feel the cold?
The musk ox is perfectly equipped to handle cold weather. As winter approaches, its hair grows even longer – almost down to its feet. During the bitter winter weather, the adults stand round the young calves to protect them from the cold.

The musk ox has been known since prehistoric times. But it almost became extinct and there are several reasons for this. Many of the young ones died of cold, or were attacked by packs of hungry wolves or bears. Most importantly, people began to use guns to hunt the animal.

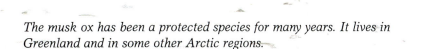

The musk ox has been a protected species for many years. It lives in Greenland and in some other Arctic regions.

The Water-Buffalo

Who is the water-buffalo's best friend?
A little bird called an oxpecker. Perched on the buffalo's back, and protected by the animal, this bird feasts on the flies, mosquitoes, lice and ticks which can poison the water-buffalo or even kill it.

The water-buffalo is a large, powerful plant eater, or herbivore. It is a peaceful animal, but it will not hesitate to attack when it feels threatened, often killing the intruder. If the wind carries the scent of an enemy towards a herd, it starts to flee, the males bringing up the rear to protect the females and young ones.

What is the buffalo's favourite pastime?
When it isn't grazing, the buffalo loves to wallow in mud for hours on end. When dry, the mud protects it from insects.

When do the males fight each other?
During the mating season, if two males want the same female they will fight to win her. They push against each other with their huge heads. The battle is over when the weaker buffalo finally lowers its head.

Different types of water-buffalo: top left, the African water-buffalo; top right, an Asian water-buffalo; left, a small water-buffalo called an anoa.

The Giraffe

How does the giraffe live?
Giraffes live in Africa in herds and spend the day in the shade of the trees. Their favourite food is the leaves of the acacia tree. The giraffe also eats grass, but it needs to spread its legs wide apart in order to reach the ground. It can go for many months without drinking any water.

Do giraffes fight each other?
Yes. In the mating season, the males fight by hooking their long necks around each other and hitting their rivals with their heads.

The mother licks the baby giraffe all over as soon as it is born. This dries the baby and helps it to get on its feet. To protect it, the mother places the baby between her hind legs, but few animals, including the lion, dare attack a giraffe.

With its long neck, the giraffe is the tallest animal in the world. It isn't unusual to find males whose heads are over 5 metres from the ground! One giraffe from the herd will keep watch whilst the rest eat. If a lion or other dangerous animal comes too near, the 'look-out' warns the others of danger.

The Okapi

◀ *The okapi has distinctive white stripes on its legs.*

The okapi feeds on roots, stems and leaves.

The okapi is the rarest animal in Africa. It lives in dense rainforests, where it hides because it is very timid. Its coat is brown, but its flanks and feet have distinctive white stripes on them. The okapi usually lives in a family group consisting of a male, one or two females, and some calves. The okapi is related to the giraffe.

Does it have horns like a giraffe?
Only the male okapi has horns. It has 2 small horns covered with 'velvet' on its forehead. These horns are not used as weapons. When it is in danger, the okapi runs away or kicks out with its sharp hooves.

Does the okapi use its tongue much?
Yes, it has a very long tongue which it uses to wash its ears and face, to catch the flies that annoy it, or to pull food into its mouth.

How does it spot its enemies?
The animal's poor eyesight does not bother it in the jungle because it has other qualities that allow it to detect the presence of an enemy: it hears the slightest sound and has an acute sense of smell.

The Stag

The stag's antlers look like a huge crown on its head.

The majestic beauty of the stag has earned it the name 'the king of the forests', but it is a wary animal. It lives in a herd, with stags in one group and females and fawns in another.

What are the stag's horns called?
The correct name for these is antlers, and in most species only male deer have them. Every year, in March, the stag sheds its antlers. These grow again in 3 to 5 months and are covered in soft skin called 'velvet'. The stag rubs its antlers against tree-trunks to get rid of the velvet. The antlers of an adult stag can be over 1.5 metres long and can weigh more than 20 kilograms.

Why do stags make so much noise?
In autumn, only the males make a noise. They are calling the females to mate with them. During this time, the stags often fight amongst themselves, using their antlers and hooves to hit their rivals. The male who wins takes many female mates.

The fawn is born in a well-hidden place and concealed in the grass. The mother licks it clean, then she leaves it alone for several days, only returning to the baby in order to feed it.

47

The Camel and the Dromedary

What are their humps for?
Their humps contain fatty tissue which is used as a food reserve. This means the animals can go without food for many days. They are also able to survive for long periods without water.

Do they ever get too hot?
No, never. Their thick coat protects them from the heat of the sun and from the cold desert nights. Besides, they are able to stay out in the sun much longer than a person can.

A simple way to remember the difference between a camel (2 humps) and a dromedary (1 hump): the word 'camel' has 2 syllables – ca-mel. And the camel has 2 humps – easy!

The camel and the dromedary are very much alike. No other animals are so well adapted to the deserts of Africa and Asia. Their eyes are protected by long lashes, their nostrils can be closed during sandstorms, and their large hooves prevent them from slipping on the sand.

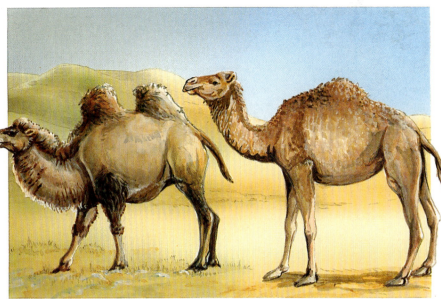

Camels and dromedaries have been domesticated for over 4000 years.

The Llama

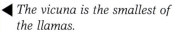
The vicuna is the smallest of the llamas.

Young llamas love to play at fighting.

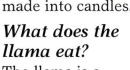

The llama is a mammal that belongs to the camel family. However, it lives in an entirely different place. The llama lives in the high mountains of South America – the Andes.

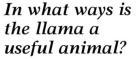

Another type of llama, the alpaca, gives long, fine wool.

In what ways is the llama a useful animal?
For the people who live in the Andes, the llama is a domestic animal. It can withstand high altitudes and very low temperatures, and can carry very heavy loads. Its wool is used to make warm clothing, its skin provides leather to make shoes and gloves, and its fat can be made into candles.

What does the llama eat?
The llama is a ruminant. It eats grass, which it does not immediately digest. Its stomach allows it to regurgitate the grass later and to chew it slowly before finally digesting it.

Why does the llama spit?
It spits in self-defence. It also acts like this when it's angry. It will spit a jet of saliva into an enemy's face.

The Sloth

The sloth lives in the forests of South America. As it hangs from the branch of a tree, it is almost invisible. Not bothering to camouflage itself, its colouring and lack of movement allow it to blend in with the foliage.

The sloth spends hours hanging on to the same branch of a tree.

Why is it called a sloth?

Sloth means laziness, and the sloth is slow – very slow! – in everything it does. It moves carefully from branch to branch as though in slow motion, and it feeds itself just as slowly. It picks leaves, then chews and digests them very slowly. The sloth preserves as much energy as possible all the time!

How does the sloth wash itself?

It never washes! That is why tiny plants grow on its fur. It is these plants that can often make the sloth look green.

What is the baby sloth like?

The baby sloth is born lazy and never lets go of its mother. It hangs on to the fur on her back for hours on end, always in the same position, whether the mother is sleeping or moving through the trees.

During the rainy season, the sloth is capable of hanging without moving for weeks. Plants grow on its fur and attract caterpillars, which the sloth often eats. When they have completed their metamorphosis, butterflies hatch on the sloth before flying away.

The Giant Anteater

How many teeth has an anteater?
It doesn't have any teeth. It uses its long tongue to catch the insects it needs for food.

Does the anteater eat only ants?
No, it also eats termites. With its keen sense of smell, it can easily find a termite mound or an anthill. It uses its strong claws to break it open, then pokes inside with its long, sticky tongue. The insects stick to this, the anteater pulls it out of the nest, and its feast begins.

The giant anteater can be almost 3 metres in length. It has a very long nose and a long tail. It lives in the forests and grasslands of South America and comes out at night to search for food.

How does the anteater use its tail?
The giant anteater's tail is long and feathery. When the animal is sleeping, or when the weather is cold or rainy, it covers its head with its tail. In this way, the anteater protects itself without having to dig a burrow.

▲ *The anteater unfolds its tongue to catch the insects it loves to eat.*

The Pangolin

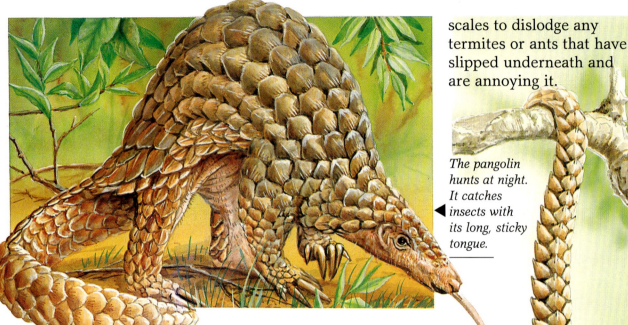

The pangolin hunts at night. It catches insects with its long, sticky tongue.

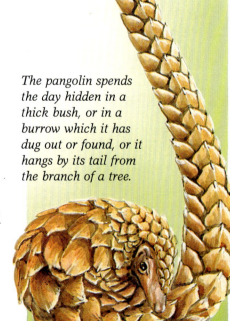

The pangolin spends the day hidden in a thick bush, or in a burrow which it has dug out or found, or it hangs by its tail from the branch of a tree.

The pangolin, also called the scaly anteater, could be confused with a reptile, but it is actually a mammal. It lives in the forests of Asia and Africa.

Is it well protected?
Perfectly, because its body is covered with sharp, overlapping scales. Only its stomach, chest and cheeks are not covered in scales.

Does it have any teeth?
No. It doesn't need teeth for eating or for defending itself. When attacked, it sometimes uses its strong claws to protect itself, but if it isn't angry it just rolls itself up into a ball. If an enemy touches it, the sharp, pointed scales stand on end to protect the animal.

Does the pangolin have a tongue?
It has a long, sticky tongue which is half as long as its body! This tongue is excellent for catching the termites and ants that the pangolin lives on. It breaks open the termite mound and pushes its tongue inside to catch the insects.

Why does the animal shake itself?
The pangolin regularly shakes itself. It flicks up its scales to dislodge any termites or ants that have slipped underneath and are annoying it.

The Armadillo

The giant armadillo has the most teeth. It lives in Central and South America.

The armadillo is a strange little creature whose entire body, except its underparts, is covered in armour. This is a horny shell connected by rings which allow the armadillo to move and to roll up into a ball. The shell is soft at birth, but quickly hardens. The armadillo lives in a burrow which it builds with two entrances.

▲
When threatened, the armadillo rolls itself up into a ball. Very few animals can kill it. Sometimes, it quickly buries itself under the nose of its enemy.

How does it find food?
With its keen sense of smell, the armadillo can detect creatures hidden deep beneath the ground. It then digs with its strong claws, thrusting its snout into the earth. In order to avoid breathing in the dust, it can hold its breath for several minutes whilst digging. The armadillo eats insects, mushrooms, roots, and even carrion.

What a strange way of swimming!
Although it is a heavy animal, the armadillo can swim and has a hidden talent. If it inflates its stomach and intestines with air, it can float! The armadillo is also capable of running along the bed of a river.

The Duck-billed Platypus...

What do they eat?
The menu of the platypus consists of worms, insects and shellfish. It catches fish with its bill. The spiny anteater, as you would expect, feasts on ants and termites, which it catches using its long, sticky tongue.

It takes only a few seconds for the spiny anteater to bury itself when it feels threatened.

The duck-billed platypus and the spiny anteater are the strangest of animals. They do not look alike, and yet they are the only two mammals in the world that lay eggs.

The platypus is an excellent swimmer. It always lives near a river or stream.

What does the platypus look like?
This shy animal has the beak of a duck, the tail of a beaver, clawed, webbed feet, and a sleek, furry body. It is no bigger than 50 cm in length. The males have a kind of poisonous claw on the heel of each hind leg.

And the spiny anteater?
This animal, also called the echidna, is a ball of spines, with clawed feet and a long, thin snout.

After mating, the female platypus digs a burrow in the river bank. Here, she prepares a nest of leaves and grass where she will lay her eggs – two or three at the most. The young are born after about 12 days.

...and the Spiny Anteater

What do both creatures have in common?
They both suckle their young and yet they have no teats. Instead, the milk oozes from folds in the mother's skin, where it is licked up by the babies. Also, both animals have an excellent sense of smell. The platypus even fishes with its eyes closed! They are the only mammals to possess an 'egg tooth'.

As soon as it is born, the baby platypus licks the milk from a fold in its mother's skin.

What is an 'egg tooth'?
This is a tiny tooth which usually only baby birds have. But these strange little animals, the platypus and the spiny anteater, are not like other animals. Their babies also have an egg tooth at the end of their snout. This allows them to break out of their eggshell. Afterwards, they lose the tooth quite quickly.

Where do these animals live?
The platypus builds its burrow near water, underneath the roots of a tree, by using its flat tail. The spiny anteater lives in rocky or wooded areas. Using its strength and its clawed feet, it can dig a hole in which to hide in a few seconds. Both animals are found in Australia and Tasmania. The spiny anteater is also found in New Guinea.

Do spiny anteaters have spines from birth?
No, the baby is completely naked when born. Because it has no spines, it grows in its mother's pouch, where it drinks the milk that nourishes it. But when the quills begin to grow – ouch! they hurt, and the mother doesn't want the baby in her pouch any more. She leaves the youngster in a safe place and brings it food to eat.

When the spiny anteater emerges from its egg, it is a grub. It grows in its mother's pouch. This pouch disappears once the baby begins to take shape.

Some Marsupials

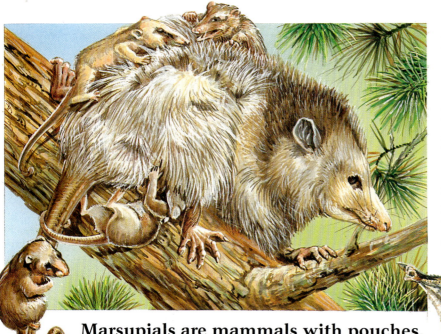

But it also has amazing teeth which quickly grow again as soon as they wear out.

The marsupial mouse
Not only does this little mouse (shown left) carry its babies on its back or on the end of its tail, it also doesn't need a suitcase. It only needs to roll its tail around a bundle of twigs to carry them.

Marsupials are mammals with pouches. When baby marsupials are born, they are tiny and not completely formed. They climb up to reach a teat in the pouch and attach themselves to it for several months. There are many types of marsupial, including kangaroos, koala bears, possums and wombats.

The wombat – a strange little animal
The wombat is a comical animal that lives in Australia. When it is frightened, it gets hiccups!

The flying possum is also called the flying squirrel.

Does the flying possum really fly?
It would be more true to say it glides, thanks to the skin that connects its hind legs to its front legs. At the age of 4 months, hanging on tightly to its mother's back, the tiny possum takes its first flying lesson.

When it has had enough sun, the wombat hides in a burrow.

The Kangaroo

When in danger, the kangaroo escapes by making jumps of almost 8 metres, travelling at nearly 50 km/h.

With its very short front legs, long, slim feet, huge hindquarters and large muscular tail, the kangaroo is the biggest of the marsupials. It lives in Australia. The wallaby is a type of kangaroo.

How does the baby get into its mother's pouch?

The baby kangaroo is born blind. It is a tiny creature, only about 2 cm long. It crawls instinctively through its mother's fur to reach her pouch. As soon as it gets inside the pouch, it attaches its mouth to a teat. It does not feed itself. Instead, the mother moves a muscle behind the teat to make the milk flow into the baby's mouth. This tiny animal will become a kangaroo in 6 months or so.

Can the kangaroo really box?

Yes, kangaroos often use their short front legs for fighting or playing amongst themselves. A kangaroo's usual method of defence when threatened is to lean back on its tail and lash out with its powerful hind legs. It will also grab hold of an enemy and suffocate it against its chest.

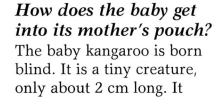

When the mother kangaroo cleans her pouch and her coat, she is about to give birth.

Whilst the mother is eating grass, the baby can also join in!

The Koala Bear

The koala bear is an excellent climber.

A little bear with a pouch and a very thick coat, the koala bear is a marsupial that lives in Australia. The koala lives in the trees and is an excellent climber. On the ground it is slow and vulnerable.

What does the koala bear eat?

It eats only the leaves and bark of certain eucalyptus trees. Other leaves are toxic and will poison it. It feeds at night and sleeps during the day.

Does it drink?

In Australia, among the Aborigines, the word 'koala' means 'the one that does not drink'. Indeed, this little animal never drinks, but sometimes it will lick the dew from leaves. Also, it is an excellent swimmer, and when it comes out of a river it will lick itself dry, so it swallows the water clinging to its fur.

A pouch for taking baby for a walk?

For 6 months, the baby koala bear remains in its mother's pouch whilst she suckles it. After that, it is carried on its mother's back for the next 2 months, before finally leaving her to start its own life.

A baby koala doesn't like being alone.

It leaps from a branch...

...and clings to the back of its mother.

Lemurs

Sifakas can make spectacular leaps from one tree to another.

In Madagascar, where they live, it is difficult to see lemurs. This is because most members of the lemur family are active at night. Lemurs look like monkeys, but their muzzle is more pointed and, above all, their brain is not as well developed. They have hands that are capable of grasping things.

What do lemurs do in the trees?

They climb up the trees to settle in the branches. There, they spend most of the day sunning themselves, with their arms and legs wide apart in order to take advantage of as much heat as possible. They also travel about looking for fruit and leaves to eat. They seize these with their mouths or eat by using their hands when sitting down. Once they have eaten their fill, lemurs settle down for a long sleep. Lemurs don't like to be alone – they live in groups.

How do lemurs talk to each other?

They have excellent hearing and communicate with one another by cries and growls. Lemurs love being together, so before going to sleep, they emit loud cries to let another group nearby know where they have decided to sleep. In this way, everyone knows where everyone else is!

Lemurs live almost entirely in the trees, except for the ring-tailed lemur which usually lives on rocky plains.

59

The Chimpanzee

Chimpanzees live in family groups in the forests of Africa. It is the animal that most resembles a human. Its hairless face is very expressive and easily shows happiness or sadness, anger or surprise. The chimp is an intelligent animal and learns quickly. Some chimps have even learned the sign language used by deaf people. Chimps can live to be quite old – sometimes as old as 50.

Why do we say the chimpanzee is intelligent?
It knows how to use tools, which it often makes itself. For example, when a chimp is thirsty, it chews a leaf, dips it in water, then squeezes it like a sponge to extract the water to drink. It also knows how to strip the leaves off a twig and use the twig to poke into an anthill so that the ants cling to the twig. Then all the chimp has to do is pull out the stick and eat the ants! It also knows how to break open fruit by using a large stone. You could say it has 4 hands, because it uses its feet as easily as its hands: it grasps things by using its toes and its thumb.

Is a baby's birth celebrated?
When a baby chimp is born, the mother immediately shows it to the other chimpanzees in the family group. In this way, it is protected.

A chimp stays with its mother until it is 5 years old. The mother teaches it all the skills it will need.

The Orang-Utan

The adult male orang-utan's large head is surrounded by a fringe of thick hair.

The orang-utan is a very cautious creature. It does not let go of one branch until its hands and feet have grasped hold of another.

The mother feeds her baby and keeps it warm by holding it close to her chest. She will look after it for the next 4 years.

The orang-utan is the largest of the tree-dwelling mammals. It has long red hair, small, close-set eyes in a bearded face, and arms which are longer than its legs. Always solitary and cautious, it lives in the forests of Borneo and Sumatra. It only comes down from the trees to drink. Orang-utans eat leaves, bark, insects and lots of fruit – they love figs and lychees.

The orang-utan's daily routine?

It gets up early in the morning and picks some fruit for breakfast. It spends the day looking for food or sleeping in its nest. Each night it builds a new nest in the trees.

Which animal is the leader?

During the mating season, the leader is the male that most of the females mate with. Adult males live separately from the females for the rest of the time, and don't make very good fathers.

Other Monkeys

uakari

spider monkey

These three monkeys live in the rainforests of South America.

The spider monkey
This monkey is a wonderful climber. It has a very long tail which it uses just like a hand. With the help of its tail, it can climb among the trees and grasp food that is out of the reach of its hands. The little ones don't hold hands – they hold tails!

The marmoset
This monkey is very small – less than 25 cm long. When it is frightened, the hair around its face stands on end. Although the mother suckles the babies, it is the male marmoset that cares for them and carries them around.

The uakari
When the uakari gets excited, its face becomes bright red and its cries, which sound like loud bursts of laughter, echo round the forest. Although its tail is really too short to help it cling to the branches, the uakari lives in the trees and rarely comes down to the ground.

marmoset

The Elephant Seal and the Walrus

The elephant seal is the largest member of the seal family.

These two animals of the polar regions are enormous. The elephant seal is three times the size of the walrus, the male weighing over 3 tonnes! Both animals are slow and clumsy on land, but in water they are very skilful swimmers.

How does the elephant seal get its name?
From its nose. The male elephant seal, which is much larger than the female, has a nose like an elephant's trunk, only not as long. This nose grows to twice its size when the animal is angry!

Why does the walrus have such long teeth?
No one is sure why they are so long. The animal uses them as supports to hoist itself out of the water. They also help it to break through ice. Some researchers think they are used by the walrus to dig in the seabed for shellfish. One thing is certain: the male uses his teeth as weapons during the mating season, when the males fight each other.

Who hunts the walrus?
The Inuit do, and have done for thousands of years. They use the flesh and the fat of the animal, and also make carvings out of the tusks.

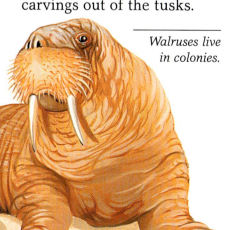

Walruses live in colonies.

Seals and Sea Lions

Seals and sea lions are marine mammals. Their smooth bodies are perfectly adapted to life in the water and they have webbed feet that look like fins. They eat fish – mostly herring – squid and shellfish. For many years, some baby seals were killed for their white fur, but now they are protected.

Is the sea lion a female seal?
No, it isn't. Although they may look alike, the two animals are quite different. A hint to recognise them: the sea lion has small ears; the seal has none. Also, the sea lion is agile and very comfortable out of the water. The seal, on the other hand, moves around the ice with difficulty.

Why do they come to land?
Both seals and sea lions come to land to reproduce.

What do they use their flippers for?
The lice in their fur makes them itch. To get rid of them, the sea lion uses its back flippers, whilst the seal scratches with its front ones. When swimming, the opposite is true: the front flippers propel the sea lion forward through the water, whilst the seal uses its back flippers.

The sea lion's enemies are the killer whale and the shark. When they are born, baby sea lions can't swim – and they hate water! Their mothers have to teach them how to control their breathing and how to co-ordinate their movements before they become the excellent swimmers that they are.

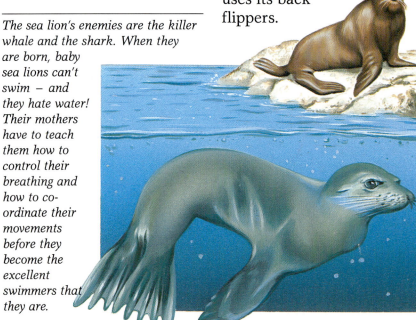

Dolphins

Dolphins are marvellous acrobats.

Dolphins live in the sea and also sometimes in fresh water. They live in groups called schools, and travel through the oceans in search of food such as squid or mackerel. They often come to the surface to breathe, using a kind of nostril on the top of their head. Dolphins are highly intelligent and love making contact with humans. The female dolphin gives birth to a calf about 11 months after mating. The baby suckles for about 6 months whilst it waits for its teeth to grow.

How do dolphins navigate?
Dolphins don't have very good eyesight. To find their way around the oceans, they send out ultrasonic signals, which are very high-pitched sounds. This dolphin language is not yet understood by humans. When the signals encounter an obstacle or a shoal of fish, they bounce back to the dolphins to tell them where it is.

Why are dolphins in danger?
Dolphins swim with the tuna fish shoals: these fish warn dolphins of danger by swimming away as soon as they spot any sharks. But the dolphins are in danger from the fishermen who catch the tuna, because many of the mammals become tangled in the nets and die. Pollution and underwater nuclear tests also threaten the dolphin's habitat.

The Killer Whale

The killer whale, or orca, is the largest dolphin. The baby killer whale is a giant from birth – it is born 2 metres long! This mammal is a ferocious hunter, roaming the oceans in groups called schools. It is easy to recognise a killer whale: it has a sleek black body with a white patch over each eye and a white stomach. It also has a fin sticking up on its back that says: Look out – danger!

What's the difference between the killer whale and other dolphins?
The killer whale is the only animal that attacks other marine mammals. It does not have a snout as other dolphins have, and it has a high curved fin and rounded flippers. The male can be almost 10 metres long – twice as long as the female.

Are they good hunters?
The best! They have a perfect method of catching prey. About 20 of them will move towards the coast in a line, trapping their prey between themselves and the rocks. Then they surround their victims and kill them.

What do killer whales eat?
They eat seals, dolphins, porpoises, seabirds and any type of fish. They also know how to tip over the ice-floes that sea lions and polar bears lie on. In packs, they will not hesitate to attack a blue whale. The killer whale's huge teeth mean it can easily tear off chunks of flesh, which it then swallows without chewing.

The killer whale will come right up to the shore to feed. Often, it attacks seals.

The Blue Whale

The baby whale remains with its mother for about 3 years.

The blue whale is the largest and heaviest animal in the world. It can be as long as 4 buses placed end to end, and it can weigh as much as 10 elephants. This marine mammal lives in cold polar waters. In winter, the females migrate to warmer water to give birth.

Does the whale have many teeth?

It doesn't have teeth. Instead, it has stiff plates, made from the same material as human fingernails, that hang down from the roof of its mouth. To feed, the whale opens its mouth and swims into a shoal of tiny shellfish, called krill. Then it closes its mouth and expels the water, trapping the krill inside. The whale swallows them in one gulp. It can eat nearly 2 tonnes of krill a day.

How big is a baby whale?

The baby whale weighs almost 2000 kilograms at birth and drinks between 90 and 200 litres of milk a day!

Why do whales sing?

No one knows. Researchers think that whales sing their haunting songs to tell each other where they are or to warn other whales of danger. But it's a mystery – no one really knows for sure.

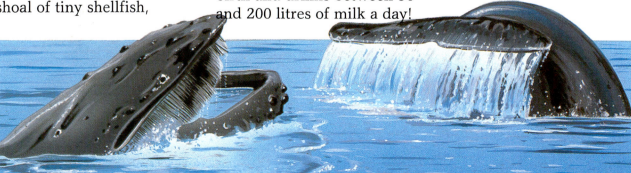

The blue whale can move at speeds of almost 30 km/h, for up to 3 hours.

The Swallow

These little birds are brave and wide-ranging travellers, crossing oceans and deserts in all kinds of weather to come to Europe for the summer to reproduce. As soon as food becomes scarce, they return to warmer lands.

How can you tell male from female?
They are difficult to tell apart, except in the spring when the female loses the feathers on her stomach. She keeps the eggs warm against her skin.

When do swallows gather together?
Swallows gather together along the telephone wires at the beginning of autumn. This means that the time for their departure to warmer lands is approaching. In spite of their small size, swallows travel thousands of kilometres, living off their reserves of fat. When they arrive at their destination, they have often lost over half their weight.

Where do swallows build their nests?
In farm buildings, under the eaves of houses, or on the cliffs – anywhere away from predators. The nest is usually cup-shaped and made from mud and straw. Most swallows will use the same nest each year.

Are the chicks often in danger?
Whilst the parents are absent from the nest, the chicks can be caught by cats or by magpies. Sometimes, a nasty fly sticks underneath their feathers and sucks their blood.

The mother swallow feeds insects to her chicks.

The Toucan

Who sits on the eggs?
Both male and female take their turn. The chicks, never more than 4 at a time, are born 2 weeks later.

In spite of its large beak, the toucan is unable to dig out its own nest in a tree-trunk.

The toucan is a bird with a large, brightly-coloured beak. Perched on a branch in the forest, it loves to play the clown. And what a noise it makes when it clacks its beak together!

Is its beak heavy?
No, it's hollow, so it's very light. But it's quite solid. A good thing, too, because one of the toucan's favourite games is to use its beak to have a swordfight with another toucan. It also uses its beak to snatch fruit from the beaks of other playmates, who then snatch it back.

So its beak is just for play?
No, the toucan also picks fruit and catches insects with it.

Some toucans nest in holes made by other birds such as woodpeckers. Since these holes are smaller than the toucan, the bird has to squeeze its way in by folding its tail over its back!

The Woodpecker

The woodpecker isn't a great traveller. It never strays far from its territory.

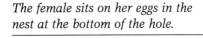
The female sits on her eggs in the nest at the bottom of the hole.

Knock, knock, knock! When you hear this noise it means a woodpecker isn't far away. Supported by its tail and clinging to the bark with its sharp claws, it taps loudly on the tree-trunks.

Does it tap for long?
For hours on end! The woodpecker has a strong beak and a strong neck which enable it to bang hard on the trunk, and a brain which seems resistant to shocks. At any rate, it never seems to get headaches!

Does it wear out its beak with drilling?
Its beak does wear out, but fortunately it grows a little more each day.

But why does it drill?
To dislodge larvae and insects from the bark. It also drills to dig out a hole. When the hole is big enough, the bird pushes in its long tongue to catch insects. A much larger hole is made for a nest.

How does the male find a mate?
The male woodpecker gets very excited – he flaps his wings, jumps, dances and makes a lot of noise. It is very difficult to miss him!

The woodpecker's feet have two toes which point backwards. These allow the bird to grip the tree-trunk very firmly. It also rests on its tail so that it doesn't get too tired.

Owls

The little owl (1) is active by day as well as by night.

The eagle owl (2) is the largest of the nocturnal hunters.

Owls are fierce hunters. They eat rodents, frogs, and small mammals. Most owls are nocturnal, but some of them hunt during the day. They have strong, sharp talons and stiff feathers around their enormous eyes. The eagle owl has tufts of feathers, like ears, above each eye. No other owl has these tufts.

The white plumage of the snowy owl helps it to blend in with the Arctic landscape.

How do owls protect their young?

Mother owls are very protective towards their chicks. It's a brave person or bird who approaches an owl's nest! The owl fluffs out its feathers and flaps its huge wings. It also has very sharp claws.

How can you spot an owl's nest?

On the ground below the nest, you will always find the feet, wings and heads of the animals the owl has eaten. It digests the bones of its prey and ejects them in the form of pellets.

The Cuckoo

Although you can often hear the cuckoo, you hardly ever see it because it is a very shy bird and keeps itself hidden away. You can recognise the cuckoo by the grey plumage of its back and wings, its striped underparts, and its long tail. Some female birds are reddish-brown.

Is the female a good mother?
No, she isn't, but she's very cunning. She lays her eggs in the nests of other birds – one egg per nest, so the other bird

doesn't notice. If necessary, the cuckoo will push another egg out of the nest to make room for hers! Then, whilst the other female is incubating her egg for her, the cuckoo goes off to enjoy herself!

Poor baby cuckoo!
Don't feel too sorry for it. The cuckoo egg is the largest in the nest and it hatches before the rest. When barely out of its shell, the baby cuckoo pushes the other eggs out of the nest whilst its foster-mother is away. Then it cheeps loudly for some food.

What does the cuckoo look like when it sings?
When its sings, the cuckoo puffs out its throat, opens its beak a little, and sways from side to side. Its drooping wings and its tail move backwards and forwards in time to its song.

The cuckoo loves insects, but its favourite food is the caterpillar.

Parrots

Why are parrots such popular pets?
Parrots are highly intelligent and can be taught to speak and to imitate sounds. Also, they love to be stroked and are very affectionate. They can live to be very old – some live to be 50 years old or even older.

Their family life?
Although parrots live together in noisy groups, the male and female mate for life. They build their nest in a hollow tree where they will raise their chicks.

The parrot family consists of many different species: macaws, cockatoos, lovebirds, lories. Parrots use their beaks like a third foot: they are excellent climbers. All parrots come from warm countries.

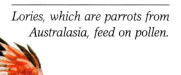

Lories, which are parrots from Australasia, feed on pollen.

Are parrots related to bats?
Not at all, although some parrots go to sleep hanging upside down from a branch. Other parrots sleep in holes in trees, or sometimes they will build a large nest out of twigs.

What do parrots like to eat?
Some species love nuts, roots and buds. Others prefer nectar and fruit. The kea, which lives in New Zealand, feeds on dead animals as well as on insects, berries, buds and honey.

The Seagull

The seagull belongs to the very large gull family. There are many different species and they live practically everywhere in the world. The seagull loves the seas and seldom ventures far from the coast.

The seagull is the largest member of the gull family.

The gull doesn't like to live alone. It lives in large colonies.

Is the seagull a good-natured bird?
No, it has a very short temper. Arguments are always breaking out between the birds when they are defending their territory. It has to be said that thousands of them live in a very small area, so things can become very cramped at times!

Why does the seagull lay eggs in odd places?
Because the eggs are often stolen. When there are no more eggs left in the nest, the female rushes off to lay some more in places which are more difficult to steal from.

Why do seagulls follow fishing-boats?
All gulls are greedy birds. They like to eat insects, worms, crabs, the eggs of other birds, and all kinds of waste. The fishermen throw overboard the entrails of the fish they have caught or the scraps from their meals. Such things are a feast for the seagull.

The Puffin

This little bird has a very apt nickname: the clown of the seas. Why? Because its brightly-coloured beak looks like the nose of a clown.

Is the puffin's beak always coloured?
No, it isn't. It is red, yellow and bright blue only during the mating season. These lovely colours disappear for the rest of the year.

The puffin is a loving and faithful little bird. It stays with its mate for life.

Where does it nest?
The puffin doesn't nest in a tree. Instead, it uses its beak and feet to dig a burrow in the cliffs, and lines it with feathers and twigs. Here, the female will lay a single egg.

The chick doesn't look anything like its parents at first. It leaves the nest after about 7 weeks.

The puffin can catch half a dozen herrings in its beak at once.

How do puffins dive?
The puffin has a technique all its own. Because it has only small wings, it isn't easy for the bird to take off. So it stands on top of a rock and launches itself into space, head first. Then, when it has gained enough speed, it rights itself and flies over the ocean. If it spots a shoal of fish – plop! it dives into the water to catch a mouthful.

The Penguin

Although it cannot fly, the penguin is a bird. It lives in large colonies around the South Pole.

Is the chick well looked after?

Yes, very. As the chick hatches, the mother places it across her feet, underneath the fold of skin so that only its head shows. The chick will be kept warm in this way for 2 months, whilst the mother feeds it with food she regurgitates. Meanwhile, the male goes off to sea to feed. When the chick is a little older, it will leave to find its own food at sea. At a year old, it is an adult.

The penguin sometimes slides down the ice on its stomach in order to reach the sea more quickly!

Are a penguin's wings for flying?

No. Penguins can't fly – at least, not in the air. But they are marvellous swimmers and look as though they are flying when under water.

Who incubates the egg?

The female lays one egg at a time. She leaves it with the male, who puts the egg under a fold of skin between his feet and his abdomen in order to protect it from the bitter cold. He stands there for the next 2 months, without moving or eating. Meanwhile, the female is at sea gathering food to give to the chick when it hatches.

The Pelican

When it spreads out its enormous wings, the pelican is larger than a motor car. Its webbed feet make it look awkward on land, but it is a graceful bird when swimming or flying. The pelican lives in large colonies near water, often in huge nests built directly on the ground.

Is its beak useful?
Yes, because it's equipped with an 'elastic' pouch that can hold up to 13 litres. To eat, the pelican lets water flow into the pouch. The fish are then trapped inside – and it swallows the lot! Pelicans always swallow fish head first.

Do pelicans have a leader when they fly?
No, each pelican takes it in turn to fly at the front. The others follow, sometimes a hundred or more of them, in a V shape. When the guide gets tired, it falls back into line and another pelican takes its place at the front.

Who looks after the chicks?
Both parents do – and they look after them very well. They take turns to hatch the eggs and feed the fledglings.

Soon after they are born, the chicks start to look for food in their parents gullets.

The Eagle

The magnificent golden eagle is the most majestic of all the eagles. It lives in mountainous regions that are difficult to reach. There, it builds a huge nest called an eyrie. The male and female take turns to feed the eaglets.

The eagle is a powerful hunter, with a wing-span of almost 2 metres.

Do eagles play games?
Yes, they like to play by dropping an animal skin or a stick when in full flight, and then catching it again far below by swooping down very quickly. Male and female eagles often play like this during the mating season. They are very skilful, and even if there is a strong wind they never miss catching their plaything.

Do they have difficulty finding food?
When hovering, the eagle's excellent eyesight allows it to spot an animal, even a small one, a great distance away. It knows how to locate the feeblest and most isolated animals. Then it swoops down on its prey, kills it with blows from its beak, and carries it off in its powerful talons.

Do the chicks get along together?
Not always. When they are young, if they haven't had anything to eat for a while, the eaglets start to fight with each other when their parents bring back food for them. The youngest chick, which is usually the weakest, risks being killed or being starved to death. Raising chicks takes a long time. Often, only one survives to adulthood. Generally, eaglets don't fly before they are 3 months old.

78

The Vulture

see when other vultures spot a dead animal.

When one vulture dives towards the corpse, all the others do the same, covering the corpse.

Vultures feed mostly on dead animals and don't kill their own prey. The bird's enormous wings mean it can hover in the air for hours whilst looking for the corpses it lives off. Vultures have a long neck, a bald head and a large hooked beak.

Which vulture is the largest?

The condor. This impressive bird, the largest flying bird in the world, lives in the Andes mountains of South America, where it spends the night among the crags and then soars on the air currents during the day. The condor eats the corpses of cattle and young animals such as fawns, and also whales that have become beached.

How do they find a corpse?

Vultures have sharp eyes and a keen sense of smell. When they are hovering above ground, they can

The digestive juices in a vulture's stomach enable it to digest bones and also the many poisonous substances found in the animal corpses it feeds off.

The Flamingo

The largest flamingo, the pink flamingo, can be nearly 1.5 metres tall. It is a magnificent bird which lives in huge colonies around lakes and ponds.

How does the flamingo catch its food?
It stamps on the mud to release the shrimps and other crustaceans that it loves to eat. Then it unravels its long neck and, with its head half hidden under the water, the flamingo searches through the mud for food. It opens its beak and traps the small crustaceans inside.

What is the pile of mud?
It's a nest. The male and female build it together. They both make pellets of mud. Then they flatten these with their large webbed feet, and gradually the nest takes shape. A hollow is left at the top of the nest in which the female usually lays a single egg. Both parents incubate the egg for a month until the chick hatches.

The chick is fed by both parents, who feed it through their beaks with a nourishing secretion from their stomachs.

Is the flamingo always pink?
Not always. In fact, when born, the chicks are greyish-white. As they get older the chick's plumage changes colour and can vary from white to pink, or even red, depending on what type of flamingo it is. The colouring of this pretty bird depends on what it eats. Its food is mostly shrimps and other crustaceans which contain the pink colour that passes into the flamingo's feathers. The bill and legs of a flamingo are usually bright red.

The Heron

Does the heron like food?
Yes, it loves to eat shellfish, fish, frogs, insects and sometimes even small rodents.

The heron is a magnificent water bird, with a slender neck shaped like an 'S', a long pointed beak, and long, thin feet. It lives in a colony called a heronry and builds its nest among reeds or in trees. For many years, the heron was hunted for the beautiful feathers that appear on the male during the mating season.

What is a cattle egret?
This is a small species of heron that is always found with herds of animals. Perched on the backs of buffaloes, bison and other creatures, it plucks the biting insects from the animals' skin and also warns the herd of danger.

Is the heron's long beak practical?
Yes, very practical indeed. The heron uses it like a pair of pincers when eating. It grips its prey so strongly that it can't escape. It also uses its beak to break open shellfish. The heron's pointed beak can also be used in defence: a stab in the eye of its enemy is the heron's way of defending itself.

The Kiwi

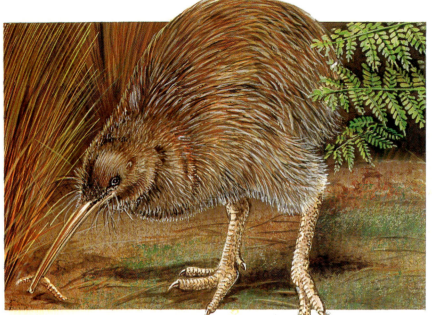

The kiwi only feeds at night. During the day, it hides in its burrow.

What an odd little bird the kiwi is! It has no tail and no wings, but it is nevertheless a bird. It runs and jumps with surprising speed, but it doesn't fly. It gets its name from the cry it makes – kiwi! kiwi! – as it searches for food.

But why does it search head-down?
The kiwi has an excellent sense of smell. It is the only bird with nostrils at the end of its beak. In order to locate the worms and insects it likes to eat, the kiwi smells at the earth and then digs it up with its beak.

Why does the female peck the male?
The female kiwi is a bit of a crosspatch. She pecks at her mate to force him to return to the nest and incubate the egg she has laid. He squats on the egg for days on end, waiting for the chick to hatch.

Where do kiwis nest?
Because kiwis don't fly, they don't live in trees. Instead, the bird uses its powerful claws to dig out a hollow in the ground. In this hollow lined with moss, the female lays her single egg.

The kiwi is no larger than a hen.

The Ostrich

With its long neck and legs, the ostrich is the largest bird in the world. It lives on the African savannah and in desert regions. It never strays far from water because it needs this to stay alive. The ostrich eats mostly plants and also swallows lots of sand to help its digestion.

Can the ostrich fly?
No, it can't but its strong legs help it to run very quickly indeed. Sometimes it reaches speeds of nearly 50 km/h. In this way, it is able to escape from lions and other predators.

Do the males often fight?
In the mating season, they fight by hitting each other with their heads and even their feet. The strongest male is the winner and he is the one who will mate with lots of different females.

Who builds the nest?
It isn't really a nest. The male just scrapes out a hole in the sand about 30 cm deep, where all the hens lay their eggs. The male and the females take turns to sit on the eggs. When the chicks are born, the male looks after them.

The Swan

The swan lands on the water feet first, flapping its wings to bring itself to a halt.

Black or white, the swan is a beautiful bird that can often be seen swimming in family groups on lakes. To take off, the swan has to run for several metres to get 'lift-off', because it is so heavy. But its weight doesn't prevent it from flying. In summer, after the mating season, the swan moults: it loses some feathers, and until new feathers have grown it is impossible for the bird to fly.

Is it good or bad tempered?

Mostly bad tempered. In spring, swans choose a territory in which to lay their eggs. If another swan or another water bird enters this area, it is likely to be bitten, beaten and driven away. Sometimes, swans try to drown each other and some of them die.

Are swans faithful to each other?

Yes, swans mate for life. Every winter, the male and female will find each other again, and stroke each other's feathers. Together, they build a new nest or enlarge the old one. Both parents look after the cygnets when they hatch.

Does the family always stay together?

No, only until the cygnets are about a year old. Then they separate from their parents and go off to start their own lives.

The Stork

The stork family consists of 17 different species. At the end of the summer, the storks that nest in Europe migrate south to the tropics because there is no food left for them. Other storks live in warm regions all the year round. The white stork, the most common one, builds its nest on the ridge of a roof, on a church tower, or even on a chimney-top.

Does the stork travel alone?
Never. Each year, storks migrate in huge flocks to spend the winter in warmer lands. During their flight, they make use of air currents and often ascend to very high altitudes. They travel together in a long line.

Does the stork sing?
The stork does not sing or call. Instead, it makes a clattering noise with its beak. During the mating season in particular, the male and female greet each other by loudly clacking their beaks together.

Storks fly with their necks outstretched.

The stork is a carnivore. It will eat anything it can get in its beak, provided it can swallow it in one gulp.

The saddle-billed stork that lives in Africa.

When the sun gets too hot, the adult protects its chicks by spreading its wings over them and sprinkling them with water.

A short tap from the beak pierces the egg
The first stork chick that hatches pecks at the other eggs in the nest. In this way, it helps the other chicks to break through their shells and emerge from their eggs.

The Peacock

What does the peacock do at night?
It climbs up into the trees and perches on the branches, where it spends the night. As day breaks, the peacock starts to make its strange cry – leon! leon!

When does the peacock display his feathers?
He displays every time he wants to be admired or whenever he wants to mate. Then, he opens his wings wide and shows off his beautiful plumage. He moves the feathers about noisily to attract a female.

The peacock has been known since ancient times. It still lives in the wild in some regions of Asia, particularly India, where it is sacred to Hindus. It isn't unusual to see peacocks perched in the trees near the temples.

Which is the male?
It's easy to recognise him. Like most species of bird, the male has the most colourful plumage. The long and extremely beautiful wing feathers of the male peacock are blue, green, purple and yellow. They look like an enormous crown around his head. The female is less striking – she has a short tail and chestnut-coloured feathers. Moreover, she does not display.

The peacock loses its colourful feathers at the end of the summer. They start to grow again towards December. Whilst moulting, the peacock appears very drab and defenceless.

Crocodiles and Alligators

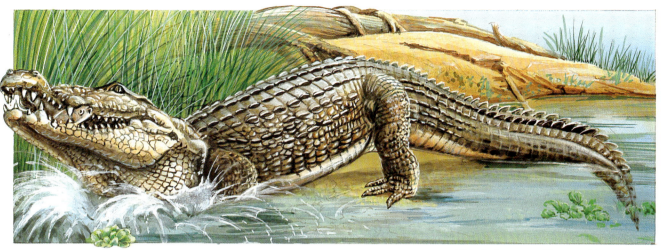

Crocodiles and alligators are the largest reptiles in the world. They look exactly as they looked in prehistoric times. They live in warm countries, where winters can sometimes be cold. They live in either fresh or salt water – anywhere where there is enough food for them. When they swim, only their eyes and nostrils are visible above water.

Crocodiles catch their prey under water by drowning them.

What do they eat?
Mostly, they eat frogs, insects, fish, toads, birds or small mammals. Some of them also like humans!

The baby crocodile uses its egg-tooth to break through its shell.

If they are really hungry, they will eat each other!

Why do they sunbathe?
They need the sunshine to warm themselves, because they are cold-blooded animals. They open their mouths wide to absorb as much heat as possible. When it gets too hot they lie in the shade.

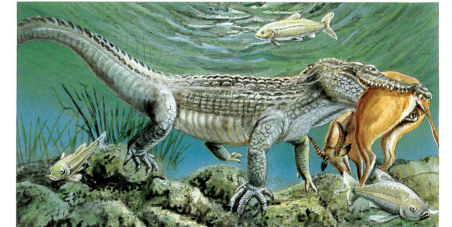

Snakes

Snakes are reptiles whose skin is cold and dry. They are covered in smooth scales. Snakes live on land or in the sea, and move about by crawling or by wriggling.

Are all snakes dangerous?
Most of them aren't dangerous to people. But some have fangs in their

A cobra ready to strike. When threatened, it can spit venom over 2 metres.

Do snakes moult?
Several times a year, a snake changes its skin because it has either worn it out or it has grown too large to fit inside it. Before moulting, snakes don't eat much, their eyes become cloudy and their skin becomes paler. They wriggle out of their old skins by rubbing against stones and branches.

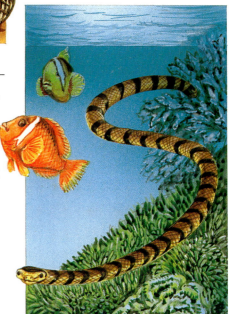

Sea snakes are excellent swimmers. They live on fish and are usually poisonous. They come to the surface to breathe, but some of them can stay under water for 8 hours without coming up for air! They lay their eggs on the shore, under rocks or in caves.

Snakes

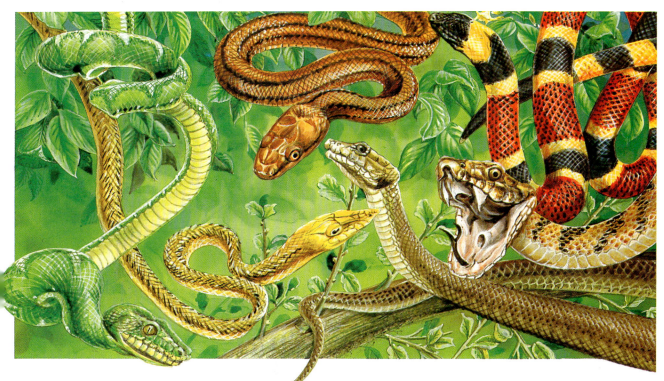

mouths which contain a pocket of venom. Poisonous snakes are dangerous as soon as they emerge from their eggs.

How do they kill their prey?
Not all snakes poison their prey. Some of them, such as the boa constrictor, wrap themselves around their victims and suffocate them. The snake swallows its prey whole, without chewing it.

It opens its mouth very wide and forces the prey towards its stomach by using strong muscular contractions.

Most snakes lay eggs. Because they are fully developed when the eggs are laid, the baby snakes easily break through their shells, and from the moment they are born they look exactly like their parents. Some snakes lay between 5 and 10 eggs, others lay 50 or more. Certain snakes, such as the asp viper, give birth to live young.

The Chameleon

The chameleon moves very slowly, always keeping its tail curled up.

The chameleon is one of the smallest species of reptile. It likes to lie along a leaf in the sun to warm itself. It is very rarely seen on the ground.

How does it see?
The chameleon's large eyes are very unusual. They can move in all directions and can move independently of each other. This is very handy for catching insects!

What is the chameleon's true colour?
It's difficult to say. The chameleon's skin changes colour according to what it happens to be sitting on. If it sits on a leaf, the animal becomes green. If it sits in the shade, it becomes brown. The chameleon also changes colour when it is angry or frightened. During the mating season, the males are brilliantly coloured.

Why does it have such a long tongue?
To capture insects to eat – and it rarely misses. However, it certainly takes its time. The chameleon watches its prey and takes careful aim. Then – whoosh! it shoots out its tongue. The tongue has a sucker on the end, to which the insect sticks. It all happens in the blink of an eye, and the chameleon then settles down to wait for another insect.

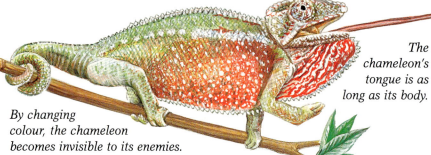

The chameleon's tongue is as long as its body.

By changing colour, the chameleon becomes invisible to its enemies.

Lizards

The agama is a lizard that, like the chameleon, can change colour.

Lizards are reptiles. Most lizards have four feet and are covered in scales. Not all lizards lay eggs in the same way. Some females lay eggs and incubate them, whilst others keep the eggs in their stomachs until they hatch.

How does a lizard defend itself?
One way in which a lizard defends itself is by breaking off its tail. A new tail then grows. The scales on the new tail are always uneven and aren't like those of the old tail.

The flying lizard leaps from tree to tree by using its 'parachute'.

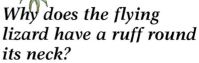

Do lizards sunbathe?
Not really, no. They are warming themselves. Because they are cold-blooded, their bodies need heat ... but not too much. When it gets too hot, they scuttle off into the shade.

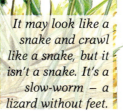

It may look like a snake and crawl like a snake, but it isn't a snake. It's a slow-worm – a lizard without feet.

Why does the flying lizard have a ruff round its neck?
To intimidate its enemies. It fluffs this out to frighten them. It also uses it as a parachute when leaping from branch to branch. At the same time, the lizard opens its mouth wide and whistles. It certainly looks and sounds very odd!

The Komodo Dragon

The Komodo dragon looks just like a prehistoric animal.

The largest lizard in the world, this animal lives on the volcanic island of Komodo in Indonesia. It can grow to over 3 metres in length, it runs very quickly and is an excellent climber. It is also a strong swimmer, although it prefers dry regions. Active by day, it returns to its burrow at night and sometimes sleeps for days.

What does it eat?
It feeds on fish, mammals and birds, but it will also eat carrion. The animals will even attack and eat each other! Young dragons climb trees to catch fledglings and eat birds' eggs.

Is it easily frightened?
If it is startled whilst in the open, where there is nowhere for it to hide, it grasps hold of the nearest upright thing it can find, which could even be someone's leg!

Does the dragon detect smells with its tongue?
Yes, the slender forked tongue of a Komodo dragon is very sensitive. It is the dragon's tongue that detects traces of animal scents on the ground and enables it to catch them. When it moves about, the lizard often shoots out its tongue to test the air for smells.

Its feet have very strong claws which, among other things, help it to dig out a cave.

The Sea Turtle

Turtles eat mostly seaweed and other vegetation, but they also like crustaceans and jellyfish. Some turtles live to be 100 years old.

The sea turtle usually lives in warm waters. Its body is covered with a heavy shell and its hind flippers help it to swim easily. It travels thousands of kilometres across the oceans to the beach where it was born. Here, the female will lay her eggs. This takes a great deal of effort because some turtles can be very heavy, weighing up to 220 kilograms.

Why does the turtle dig two holes before laying her eggs?

Whilst laying her eggs, the turtle gets very tired. So, for protection, she digs a large hole in which to hide herself, and then a smaller hole in which to lay her eggs. During this time, the males wait for the females at the water's edge.

Who incubates the eggs?

After laying her eggs, the female covers them with sand and leaves the eggs for ever! It is the sand, warmed by the sun, that actually incubates the eggs. When the eggs hatch, the baby turtles try to get to the sea, but very few of them reach it because lizards, crabs, wild cats or seabirds catch them to eat. And when they do reach the sea, sharks are waiting for them.

The turtle lays a hundred or so eggs each time.

For the baby turtles, the trek towards the sea is very dangerous. Few of them survive to reach the water.

Frogs and Toads

Frogs live near water. Because of their webbed feet, they can swim very quickly. The tiny tree frog has suckers on its feet so that it can climb up the trees where it spends most of its time. Some frogs are very brightly coloured, and these are often highly poisonous. Toads are usually brownish in colour and their skin is covered in warts. Both animals have long, pointed fingers which help them to grasp their food.

What do they eat?

Frogs and toads mainly eat insects which they catch by using their long, sticky tongues. Some of them also eat small rodents or earthworms, which they hold between their fingers. When they swallow their food, a muscle pulls their eyeballs down into the roof of the mouth, making the creature blink as it swallows.

Only male frogs and toads sing, usually during the mating season. They puff out their throats like balloons.

How does the frog protect itself from its enemies?

Some frogs bury themselves in the ground and some disguise themselves as leaves or stones. Others secrete a strong venom that paralyses the enemy. There are also frogs whose highly-coloured skin is deadly poisonous.

When resting, some toads look just like stones.

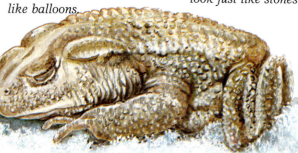

How do frogs reproduce?

A little while after they have been laid, the eggs start to develop: they become larger (1), with a head at one end and a tail at the other. After about a week, a tiny tadpole hatches out. It has neither eyes nor mouth. Instead, it has a sucker which it uses to attach itself to plants (2). After two or three days, the eyes and mouth appear (3), whilst the sucker gradually disappears. The tadpole eats a lot of plants – it is very hungry! It soon develops two legs at the base of its tail and these grow very quickly (4). Then the front legs appear, the lungs develop and the mouth changes shape (5). During this time, the tadpole uses the reserves of food stored in its tail, which becomes smaller as the nourishment it contains passes into the tadpole's blood. The eyes get bigger and bigger and the tadpole turns into a frog. It now starts to make short trips out of the water (6).

The little frog now takes on its proper shape. It grows so quickly that it has to shed its skin many times.

During the mating season, the water plants become covered with thousands of eggs.

The Sea Horse

The sea horse attaches itself to vegetation by its tail.

Although its head resembles that of a horse, this tiny creature is a fish. Its body is covered in bony rings. It has a transparent fin on its back and a tiny fin underneath. The sea horse lives among the floating vegetation of the warmer oceans. It is the only fish that swims in an upright position.

Is the sea horse a good swimmer?

No, it swims slowly and with difficulty, so it usually floats along on the current. When it wants to travel about, it unravels its tail, draws itself up straight and moves the fins on its back from side to side.

What does it eat?

The sea horse's jaws are long and thin, just like a pipe. It eats only minute marine animals: tiny fish and small crustaceans. It doesn't chew them because it hasn't any teeth. Instead, it sucks them into its mouth as they swim past, just like a vacuum cleaner!

Does the male sea horse really give birth?

During the mating season, the male and the female swim closely together, facing each other. In this way, the female can easily slip her eggs into the pouch that the male has on his stomach. Here, he will care for the eggs until they hatch. So, in the sea horse world, the father really does give birth!

The tiny babies are transparent when they are born and look exactly like their parents.

The Eel

This marvellous creature is a great traveller. The eel's long voyage begins in the ocean where it is born, continues in the freshwater rivers where it spends its adult life, and ends in the sea where it dies exhausted after spawning. It is very difficult to keep track of the eel because it changes its appearance so many times.

Where are eels born?
The eels of Europe and North America are born in the Sargasso Sea, which is an area of the Atlantic Ocean.

Where do eels live?
When they hatch, eel larvae look like transparent ribbons. It takes about 3 years for them to cross the Atlantic. A metamorphosis follows and they now take on a more eel-like appearance. These young eels, called elvers, migrate towards the freshwater streams where they will remain for the next 10 years or so, growing fatter and larger. Then they leave the river.

Where do they die?
Mature eels travel back to the Atlantic Ocean where they were born. Here, they will lay their eggs and die. Truly a voyage with no return.

Eels' skin is smooth, with scales that are almost invisible.

The eel larva is transparent, the elver is a yellowish colour, and an adult eel is silvery-grey.

The Salmon

People have tried to help the salmon on their journey by building 'fish ladders' on some rivers. Using these, the salmon can bypass waterfalls and dams more easily.

When the time comes for it to reproduce, the salmon begins a long and dangerous journey. For 4 years the fish has lived in the cold northern oceans, which it then leaves, and, without feeding or stopping on the way, miraculously finds its way back to the place where it was born, in a freshwater stream.

How do salmon find their way home?
No one knows. Perhaps it's an accident, but most people think it is because the salmon has an incredible memory. From its birth, the fish has forgotten neither the journey from its birthplace nor the smell of the river where it was born.

Who builds the nest?
The female. She scoops out a hole in the gravel on the river bed by turning over on her side and flapping her tail. There, she lays her eggs, which the male immediately fertilises.

Look out! Danger!
The salmon encounters many dangers during its journey: killer whales, seals, fishermen, dams and pollution, not to mention the ordeals lying ahead of it in the rivers it must swim up to reach its birthplace. At last, using all their energy, the salmon mate. Once the eggs have been laid and fertilised, the male and female die exhausted.

The newly-hatched salmon, called a fry, has a yolk sac which it feeds off after it hatches.

The Shark

blue shark

hammerhead

White sharks, blue sharks, hammerhead sharks, whale sharks, tiger sharks – there are lots of different kinds. The smallest is the devil shark and the largest is the whale shark. In spite of its size, this huge animal eats only fish. A shark's body is streamlined and its strong tail propels it easily through the water. The shark isn't a mammal – it's a fish.

Does the shark have any friends?
Surprisingly, yes. Often, tiny fish swim around the shark. They feed off the morsels of food that the shark leaves. Other fish actually swim on top of the shark and clean its skin.

A shark has good eyesight. It can even see the colours on the surface of the water.

How does the shark reproduce?
Some sharks lay eggs that are enclosed in a pouch and deposit them on the ocean floor. Some keep the eggs in their stomachs until they hatch. Others give birth to well-formed young, just as mammals do.

Is a lost tooth a problem?
Not at all. Sharks have many rows of sharp, pointed teeth which never stop growing. When a tooth falls out, another one is always ready to take its place.

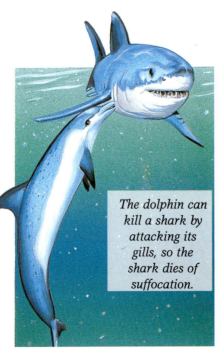

The dolphin can kill a shark by attacking its gills, so the shark dies of suffocation.

Strange Fish

Some very odd creatures live in the sea. Here are some strange fish.

Why is the porcupine fish called the sea hedgehog?

The porcupine fish is unique. It doesn't look like any other fish. Its skin is covered in lots of spines, just like a hedgehog. When it is startled, or when it feels threatened, the porcupine fish swallows lots of water and swells up like a balloon in order to frighten its enemies.

Why does the archer-fish spit?

The archer-fish has excellent eyesight. Whilst under water, it can catch insects or spiders sitting on leaves on the river bank. It spits a jet of water in the direction of its prey, which loses its balance and falls off the leaf. All the archer-fish has to do then is swallow it!

The mouth of the archer-fish is just like a water pistol!

The porcupine fish turns into a spine-covered ball when it thinks it is in danger.

Is the stonefish (left) playing hide and seek?

The stonefish is an expert at disguise. It lies on the sand between the rocks, where it can see but cannot be seen. Any fish that swims close to the stonefish had better watch out, because it will be swallowed up in a single gulp! The stonefish is also very dangerous to humans. It has poisonous spines, and if you step on the fish it can kill you.

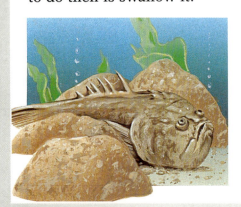

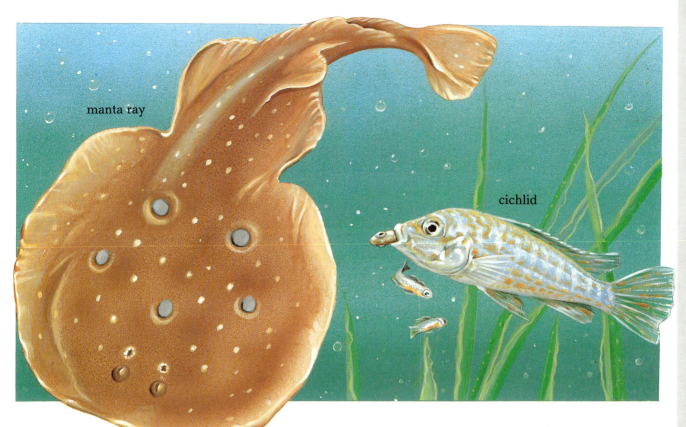

Who is the 'devil' of the seas?

The manta ray, also called the devil ray. This huge fish lives in tropical seas and uses its enormous fins, called wings, to swim at great speed through the water. It is the only member of the ray family that can jump right out of the water. But in spite of its frightening appearance, the manta ray is harmless to humans.

Where does the mother cichlid keep her babies?

In her mouth, but she doesn't swallow them. In fact, she is protecting them. The baby fish swim in a shoal around their mother. At the first sign of danger, the babies rush to hide in her mouth.

The stickleback – a fish that builds a nest!

It's true. The male stickleback builds his own nest, made from the roots and stems of water plants, on the river bed. He leaves a hole in the middle so the female can get in. She lays her eggs there and goes away again. The male cares for the eggs and looks after the baby fish when they are born. He's a very good father!

The Starfish

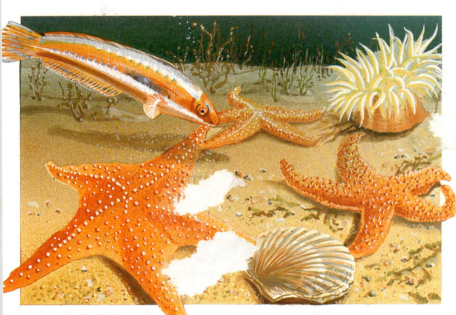

The starfish uses its five arms and flexible body to move through the water. It moves across the ocean floor on its stomach. Suckers on its feet help it to move forward.

Where is the starfish's mouth?

The mouth of a starfish is situated in the middle of its stomach, between its arms. It does not have teeth because it doesn't need them. Instead, it feeds by pushing its stomach out through its mouth! The starfish seizes its prey – a mussel, for example – and wraps itself around the shell. Then it pulls the shell apart slightly and pushes its stomach through the crack, to surround the mussel. The stomach of a starfish secretes a substance that turns the mussel flesh into liquid, making it easier to digest. Afterwards, the starfish withdraws its stomach. This feast can take as long as 15 hours!

Under its arms the starfish has thousands of tiny feet, each one ending in a sucker. These are what help it to hold on to the shellfish it feeds on.

What else can the starfish do that's unusual?

If a starfish loses one of its arms, it's no problem – a new one will grow! Some starfish can reproduce by breaking off their own arms. This arm will then grow into a new starfish. Even a starfish that has been cut in two will grow into two separate starfish.

Does the starfish eat a lot?

Yes, it does – in fact, it's quite greedy. It loves prawns, mussels, oysters, scallops, clams, snails and sea urchins. The smaller molluscs are usually swallowed whole. Some starfish live on coral reefs and feed on the coral.

Some Molluscs

It is difficult to believe that the cuttlefish, the garden snail, the mussel and the octopus are related. However, all these animals belong to the extensive mollusc family. Molluscs come in lots of different shapes and sizes. Some of them are tiny; others are huge. The bodies of all molluscs are soft and are covered in slime, or mucus. Most molluscs make a shell to protect themselves. Many of them live in the sea, some live in fresh water and others live on land.

Where are the cuttlefish's arms?
The cuttlefish (shown above) has 10 arms, 2 of which are longer than the others. It keeps these long arms rolled up in a pocket behind its eyes! It shoots them out like a spring to seize its prey. When danger threatens, the cuttlefish half buries itself in the sand and takes on the colour of its surroundings.

Does the scallop really have eyes on stalks?
Yes, it does. It has about a hundred eyes, positioned on the end of little tentacles, which keep a look-out all around. In order to escape from danger – a hungry starfish, for example – the scallop snaps the two halves of its shell together. This forces the water out of the shell and causes it to shoot forward, away from danger.

If one of the scallop's blue eyes is broken off, it will immediately grow another in the same place.

More Molluscs

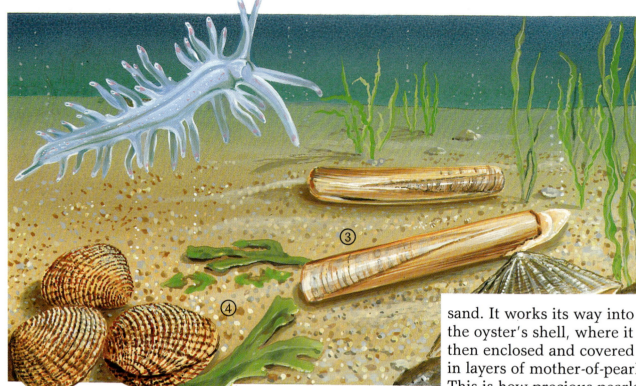

Do mussels (1) travel a long way?
No, because they spend most of their lives clinging to a rock. Mussels glue themselves to rocks by secreting fine threads from a gland in the foot. They can break these threads and make new ones, and can extend them a bit further and move to another rock, but they never go very far.

Is there a pearl in every oyster (2)?
No. Only one type of oyster produces pearls. All that is needed is a tiny grain of sand. It works its way into the oyster's shell, where it is then enclosed and covered in layers of mother-of-pearl. This is how precious pearls are formed.

Does the razor-shell (3) play hide and seek?
The razor-shell buries itself in the sand and is very difficult to catch. In this way it protects itself and also shelters from the sun, which is likely to dry it up when the tide goes out.

Other molluscs that live in the sand:
cockles and clams (4), to name just two, protect themselves by burrowing in the sand. You can tell where they are from a little hole in the sand.

The snail is an hermaphrodite, which means that it is both male and female at the same time. But in spite of this, two snails can mate so that fertilisation takes place. Fifteen days later, the eggs appear from an opening behind the feelers.

by muscles. The snail produces a kind of slime, called mucus, which helps it to travel easily along the ground.

Where does a snail spend the winter?
In its shell. It makes the shell airtight by secreting a white mucus to seal it up. During the winter, the snail's body slows down completely and wakes up again in spring. Some desert snails can wait in a dormant state for 3 or 4 years until the rains begin to fall.

Is the snail a carnivore?
Generally speaking, snails are plant eaters, but there is a meat-eating variety that lives in Australia. This species feeds on other snails and also on earthworms.

What does a slug eat?
It eats cabbage leaves, lettuces and the tender shoots of young plants. It also likes poisonous mushrooms and toadstools. Some slugs live in the sea and feed on sea creatures such as sponges and barnacles.

Do baby snails look like their parents?
Not completely, because the babies' shells are transparent, but they harden very quickly. Snails grow at different rates, depending on what species they are, and as they grow they make their shells bigger. In filling the opening, they copy the design of the original shell exactly – an astonishing feat.

Does the snail have a tongue?
The snail has a tongue which acts as a grater. It is equipped with rows of thousands of little teeth, which grow again as soon as they are worn out. The snail uses them to nibble on leaves.

How do snails move?
The snail uses a very muscular 'foot' underneath its body to crawl along. The foot is attached to the shell

Slug

105

Some Crustaceans

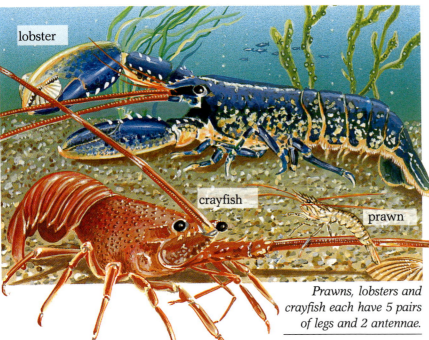

Prawns, lobsters and crayfish each have 5 pairs of legs and 2 antennae.

Most crustaceans live in either salt water or fresh water, but some of them, such as the woodlouse which hides under tree bark or stones, live on land. Crustaceans get about by swimming or walking, and some of them cling to rocks or to other sea creatures.

Their eggs turn into larvae before changing into adults through metamorphosis. In general, the body of a crustacean is protected by a hard shell, called a carapace. When the shell gets too small, it is shed. This is known as moulting. Another shell appears immediately. It is soft at first, but it hardens in time.

Is the crayfish a type of lobster?

No, it isn't. Although they both belong to the same family, they are different creatures. It is easy to tell them apart – they both have 2 long antennae, or feelers, but the lobster also has 2 large, powerful pincers, which it uses to catch its prey and to crush it.

When is the crab in danger?

When it has just moulted, because its new shell does not harden straight away. It stays soft for some time and does not protect the crab. So the crab has to hide.

Crabs lay eggs which hatch into tiny larvae. These larvae will undergo many changes and moultings as they grow.

Plankton is a mixture of microscopic living organisms: vegetal plankton is made up of algae, and animal plankton includes tiny jellyfish, fish eggs and crustacean larvae.

More than 10 legs?

In addition to their 10 legs, crabs have numerous other claws which are used for various purposes – breathing, chewing food, moving eggs, etc.

How do crabs catch their food?

Some gather their food through the tiny hairs in their claws. The food stays trapped as though in a sieve, and can then be eaten. Other crabs, which are bigger, catch prey by using their pincers.

Does the fiddler crab play the fiddle?

No, of course not, but it makes a high-pitched sound by rubbing its enormous front claw against its shell. Only the males have this large claw, and if it is broken off, a small new claw appears in its place. The other front claw then grows to become the large claw. The crab also waves its huge claw to attract passing females. The fiddler crab is tiny, its body measuring less than 4 cm across.

Where do freshwater crayfish live?

They live in ponds, lakes and rivers. The female crayfish is smaller than the male. During ovulation, the crayfish keeps its black eggs attached to its abdomen. It keeps them this way for about 6 months. Then the tiny greyish-white crayfish with a soft shell will hatch.

Is plankton useful?

Very. It provides food for crustaceans, whales and other sea creatures.

fiddler crab

When in danger, the crayfish runs backwards!

The Sea Anemone

Experimental studies have shown that the anemone is unable to survive without help from the clown fish.

Red, green, blue or pink, depending on the species, the sea anemone is a marine animal. It clings to rocks and other hard surfaces with its suckers. Some anemones burrow into the sand or mud. Although they can creep along very slowly if necessary, sea anemones rarely move.

Does the anemone have any friends?

The sea anemone has a good friend called the clown fish. This fish is immune to the anemone's poison, which means it can move through and brush against the anemone's tentacles without being stung. Scientists have discovered that the skin of the clown fish produces a substance which protects it from the anemone's sting. When danger threatens the clown fish, it hides itself in the middle of the anemone's tentacles. As a way of thanking the anemone, the clown fish's beautiful colouring attracts prey which the anemone swallows. Hermit crabs are also the anemone's friends.

What if a fish touches an anemone?

Any fish that touches the tentacles is injected with a deadly poison that paralyses the fish and prevents it from moving. Then the anemone grasps the fish with its tentacles and draws it towards its mouth so it can eat it.

When disturbed, the sea anemone pulls its tentacles down into its mouth. It then looks just like a round lump on the rock.

The Octopus

After laying her eggs, the female octopus anchors them to the floor of her cave. She looks after them for the next two months until they hatch. During this time she does not feed. After the eggs hatch, she leaves them.

The octopus is a mollusc. It has 8 arms, called tentacles, which are covered in suckers. The octopus lives in the sea, where it spends most of its time in a cave which it protects by a wall of stones, empty shells or pieces of wood. There are both giant octopuses and tiny ones.

What does the octopus do when danger threatens?

It releases ink to blind whatever is threatening it, and then it flees. It is difficult to find again afterwards! Octopus ink is special: just one squirt of it and the enemy loses its sense of smell.

Why does the octopus have so many arms?

It needs them to get about, to catch its prey of shrimps, crabs and mussels, to feed, to investigate its surroundings, to move stones. To do everything, in fact.

Is the octopus patient?

Yes, very. When it captures a big lobster, the octopus doesn't eat it straight away because the shell is too hard. Instead, it waits until the lobster moults. Then, when the lobster is soft, the octopus eats it.

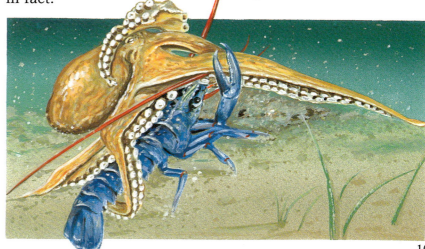

The Piranha

Do piranhas swim alone?
The danger with piranhas is that they never swim alone. Sometimes there are several thousand of them. When piranhas hunt in a shoal, they all attack the same prey and can strip it to the bone in a few minutes.

The piranha is a very bloodthirsty fish indeed! It spends its time hunting in the rivers of South America, where it lives. It has an enormous appetite and needs to have lots of prey around it all the time so that it can feed whenever it likes.

Is the piranha a big fish?
No, it is usually about 30 cm in length, but some scientists think it is more dangerous than a shark.

When they smell blood, piranhas appear in their thousands!

What are its teeth like?
As pointed as daggers and as sharp as razors! The piranha has a powerful lower jaw, equipped with sharp, pointed, triangular teeth. The teeth in the upper jaw are also formidable, but they are smaller. They slot in perfectly between the points of the lower teeth.

The Ladybird

Contrary to popular belief, the spots do not indicate a ladybird's age.

Mating.

Laying eggs.

Depending on what kind it is, a ladybird can be red, orange, yellow or black, with spots of a contrasting colour. It has two pairs of wings – a delicate inner pair protected by a hard outer pair.

Does the ladybird like to eat?
It certainly does! It is most hungry when it is a larva. Usually, the ladybird lays its eggs where there are lots of greenfly. This means the larvae will be surrounded by their favourite food. Afterwards, in the adult stage, the ladybird eats the same things. The ladybird has jaws for grinding – and it uses them! It is capable of eating between 30 and 40 greenfly a day.

How does the ladybird avoid being eaten by its enemies?
The ladybird's blood has a very unpleasant taste which only a few birds can tolerate. The others leave the ladybird well alone.

The eggs hatch and larvae appear.

The tiny larvae are very hungry indeed.

The larva attaches itself to a stem and stops eating. Then it turns into a pupa. Finally, a tiny ladybird without spots emerges.

The colour and the spots appear a little later.

Ants

Aphids secrete a sugary substance that ants love. Some ants keep 'herds' of aphids in their nests so they always have a supply of their favourite food!

Do ants bite?
Some species do, yes. There are even some whose bite can be very painful and dangerous.

What is an ant's essential tool?
Its jaws, or mandibles. It uses them to dig tunnels, to cut and carry things, to bite, etc.

Ants are small black, brown or red insects which are always very busy. They live in colonies in an anthill, which can be found in a field, under rocks or in a tree.

What happens if one ant meets another ant?
They recognise each other by smell and in this way they know whether they belong to the same anthill. They also collect food with the help of their sense of smell. Ants smell by using their feelers, or antennae.

When a hunter ant returns to the anthill, it feeds the worker ants who have stayed behind in the nest. They pass the food from mouth to mouth.

Some honey ants store honeydew in their stomachs. They hang from the roof of the nest and feed the honeydew to other ants when stroked.

Some ants have wings –
these are the future queens and the males. After mating, the males die. Each queen loses her wings and builds an anthill, where she will continue to lay eggs until the end of her life.

Insects

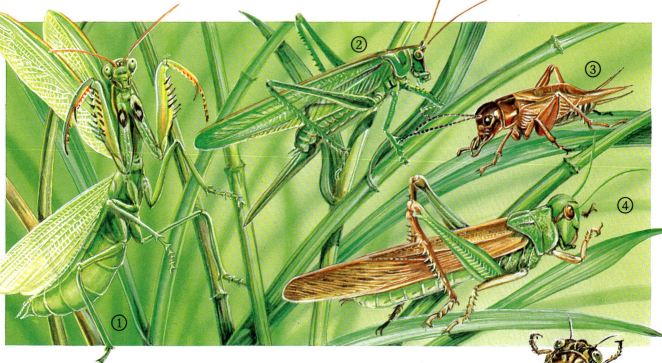

Does the praying mantis (1) have a hearty appetite?
Yes, it's ravenous! The praying mantis takes its prey by surprise. If it gets hold of a cricket or a grasshopper, it won't let go. It eats almost all of its victim. After the meal, its stomach is twice its normal size!

Does the cricket (3) sing all day?
No, only at night during the summer. The male cricket positions himself at the entrance to his burrow. Then he scrapes his wings together rapidly to attract a female.

Are the grasshopper (2) and the locust (4) the same?
No, they should not be confused with one another. The grasshopper has bigger antennae than the locust, and the female's abdomen ends in a long point. The grasshopper is a flesh eater, whilst the locust eats mainly plants.

How does the cicada (5) sing?
It contracts and expands its stomach muscles thousands of times a second, so that its skin vibrates rapidly. It is the male who produces this sound in summer.

Insects

The strange life of the cockchafer beetle (6)
The white larvae live underground for several years — 3 to 5 years, depending on the climate. They eat the roots of all kinds of plants and cause a great deal of damage. After metamorphosis, they emerge from the ground as adults, but from then on they have only a few months to live.

Where does the monarch butterfly (7) go?
In autumn, the monarch butterfly travels to warmer countries where it spends the winter. In spring it flies north again. It is the only migratory butterfly to return to the place of departure at the end of its journey. The journey covers thousands of kilometres and lasts for the whole of the monarch butterfly's life.

Why does the glow-worm (8) shine?
The female glow-worm hasn't any wings, so in order to attract the male, she raises up her abdomen to reveal her luminous organs. She flashes signals to the male to show him where she is.

Which insect is an acrobat (9)?
The click beetle. Its legs are too short to turn it over when it falls on its back. But luckily it is able to hurl itself into the air with a loud "click" and land on its feet.

What is the bluebottle (10) looking for?
It is searching for meat, but not for itself...for its larvae. When it finds a piece of meat, it lays its eggs there. They hatch a day later. The larvae which emerge are called maggots. They produce a substance that makes the meat soft enough for them to eat.

Does the centipede (11) really have 100 legs?
Nowhere near! The best-known centipede has 42 legs, which help it to move quickly across the ground. You should not touch a

Insects

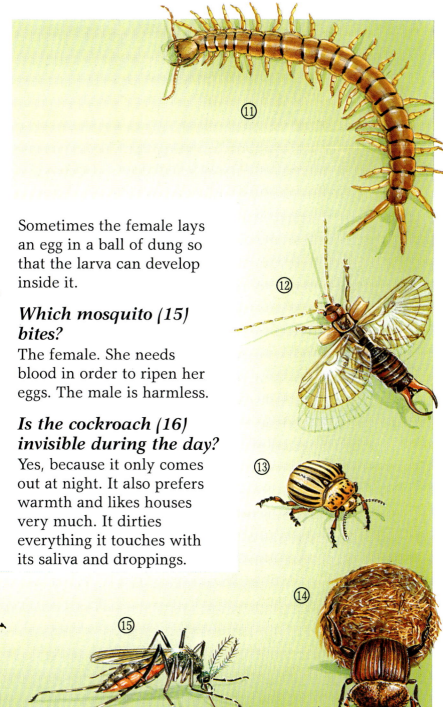

centipede because its bite can be as painful as a wasp sting.

How did the earwig (12) get its name?
Earwig comes from the Anglo-Saxon meaning 'ear creature'. This was because people believed that earwigs crawled into their ears when they were sleeping. But this is just an old superstition.

Why don't farmers like the Colorado beetle (13)?
Colorado beetles feed particularly on the leaves, roots and shoots of potatoes. They cause serious damage to the potato crop.

What game does the dung-beetle, or scarab, (14) play?
When it smells a pile of dung, the beetle hurries towards it. It rolls pieces of the dung into balls and buries it for food.

Sometimes the female lays an egg in a ball of dung so that the larva can develop inside it.

Which mosquito (15) bites?
The female. She needs blood in order to ripen her eggs. The male is harmless.

Is the cockroach (16) invisible during the day?
Yes, because it only comes out at night. It also prefers warmth and likes houses very much. It dirties everything it touches with its saliva and droppings.

Termites

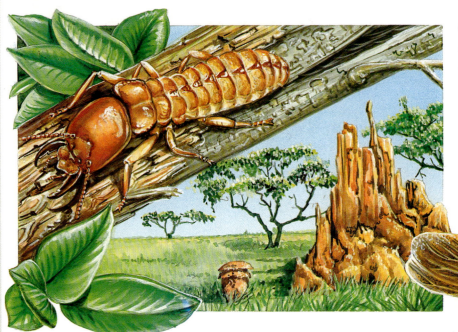

Termites are insects which eat mainly wood. They live in a highly organised society with a king, a queen, workers and soldiers. Some termites build colonies underground, but most live in a mound called a termitary.

Who builds the termite mound?
The termites themselves. Some termite mounds can be 4 to 6 metres high. They are as hard as rock, and up to one million termites can live in them.

What do the king and queen do?
Once a year, young kings and queens fly off to mate and start new colonies. After they have mated, they lose their wings and never leave the nest again.

What do the workers do?
They work constantly. They dig the tunnels, look after the young and hunt for food.

And what about the soldiers?
They defend the queen and the termite colony. Although they are blind, they are able to detect their enemies by using their sense of smell. They defend themselves by using their powerful jaws or by discharging a sticky substance.

The queen's abdomen may be up to 10 cm in length. She cannot feed herself and worker termites bring food for her. Some queens lay one egg a second, 24 hours a day, for 10 years!

Wasps

A paper nest?
Yes, some wasps make their nests out of wasp paper, which they make by chewing rotten wood or plant roots and mixing this with their saliva. The most common type of nest has a central column with several

Solitary wasps build different types of nests.

There are lots of different species of wasp which live either in colonies or on their own. The females do not hesitate to sting when they are in danger, but wasps are useful because they kill lots of harmful insects. Wasps' bodies are often yellow with black patches.

What does the spider wasp hunt?
It hunts spiders – even tarantulas! – and paralyses them with a sting. Then it drags the spider to its nest and lays an egg on top of it. Then it closes up the nest and goes away. The juicy spider provides a lovely meal for a baby spider wasp!

The mason wasp lays its eggs on a caterpillar, which it has paralysed with a sting and which will be used as food for the larvae when they hatch.

The hornet is a type of large wasp that lives in colonies. Its sting is very painful.

floors around it made out of little boxes which are open at the back. Everything is surrounded by a kind of bag made of wood pulp. Some wasps construct nests from clay.

Bees

The gatherer bee sucks up the nectar with its proboscis and transports pollen with its feet.

Bees are very organised insects that live in colonies in a hive, either a natural hive or one built by a person. They also set up home in tree trunks or in rock crevices. Bees make honey.

Are bees generous?
Very! They never keep their food to themselves, but share it with all the other bees in the hive.

Who lives in the hive?
There is a single queen, several drones (males who do not work) and the workers – about 50 000 bees in all. Each bee has a particular role to play.

Day and night, the queen lays an egg in each empty cell. She lays more than 1000 eggs each day!

The workers build the various cells in the hive with the help of the wax they secrete. ▶

How do bees understand each other?
Bees talk to each other by dancing! In flight, they perform a kind of ballet by moving their wings and their bodies faster or slower. All these movements have a particular meaning. For example, bees dance to show where food can be found.

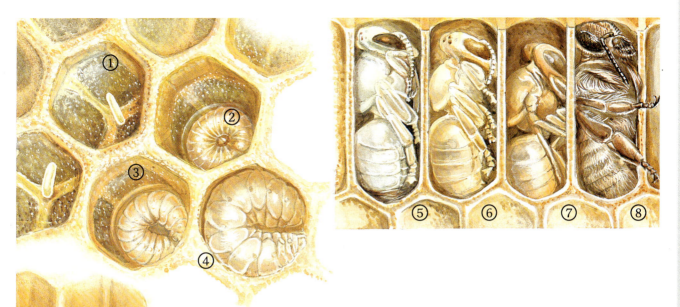

Development of the eggs

When the eggs have been laid by the queen, they are no more than 3 mm long (1). The nurse bees, who are in charge of keeping the eggs at the right temperature, now move into the cells. After 3 days, tiny larvae emerge (2). They develop very quickly (3 and 4). At first the worker bees feed them with a special substance called royal jelly. Three days later they are fed with a mixture of honey and pollen, called bee-bread. After about a week, the workers seal up the cells with wax. The larvae will now change into pupae, and then into young bees (5, 6, 7 and 8). Finally, after 21 days, the bees break through the waxy covering using their mandibles and emerge (9), quite damp, from the cells. During their life in the hive, the bees will change jobs several times and may be nurse bees, guardians, ventilators (who aerate the hive), etc.

What happens to the queen bee?

The few larvae that are destined to become queens are given the biggest cells and are fed only on royal jelly. When one of these young queens emerges, the old queen leaves the hive with the drones and many of the workers. This group, known as a swarm, clusters on a branch whilst scout bees look for a place where a new colony can be created.

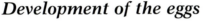

◀ *A swarm in a tree.*

Butterflies and Moths

What are the stages in a butterfly's life?
The butterfly lays an egg on a plant (1). The larva which emerges (2) is called a caterpillar (3). It moves using its feet equipped with suckers. The caterpillar sheds its skin 4 or 5 times as it grows (4). Using special glands, it spins a silky thread. Then it hangs from a branch or buries itself in the ground and turns into a chrysalis (5) (moths weave a silky cocoon). After numerous transformations (6), which can take several years, an adult butterfly emerges from the chrysalis (7 and 8).

Butterflies and caterpillars look like two completely different insects, and yet they are one and the same. How can this be? It's because the butterfly changes its appearance throughout its life. The caterpillar is just one of the stages in its life.

What does the butterfly do when it emerges from its chrysalis?
It can't fly straight away because its wings are damp and weak, so it stretches out its wings to dry them.

Do butterflies and moths have enemies?
Yes, enemies include some solitary wasps, which paralyse the caterpillars in order to lay their eggs on them and feed their larvae. Other enemies are spiders, which spin webs to catch butterflies, and bats, which eat moths.

How do they defend themselves?
In order to hide, butterflies stay still with their wings closed. The bright colours of some butterflies act as a warning that they taste unpleasant. The cleverest ones disguise themselves as poisonous butterflies by assuming the same colouring. Others camouflage themselves as leaves.

What do they eat?
As soon as it emerges, the caterpillar eats its empty egg. Then it feeds on leaves, plants and fruit, through which it tunnels holes. Some love to eat cloth. The chrysalis doesn't eat anything. When it is an adult, the butterfly likes flower nectar and fruit juice, which it sucks up with its proboscis. It is a useful insect: it carries pollen from flower to flower thus helping pollination.

Spiders

Spiders have eight legs, often equipped with suckers and covered in hairs, a body without bones, and venomous fangs, though most of them are harmless to man. Spiders are not insects: they are arachnids.

Different stages in the creation of a spider's web.

What does a spider's house look like?

Many spiders spin webs using damp silk thread that emerges from their abdomen. The silk hardens in the air and the web becomes a food store. Some spiders build burrows with a thick web as a front door. Others live under water, in a silk web filled with air bubbles. The bubbles gradually expel the water from the web so that the spider can breathe.

How do spiders catch their prey?

Spiders attack in different ways, depending on what type they are. Some jump on their prey, others shoot hairs from their back at their prey, and others spit venom. Most spiders wait patiently in a corner of their web, or at the bottom of their burrow, until their prey gets caught in the web. The movement of the threads alerts the spider that its meal awaits!

What do spiders eat?

Spiders are useful creatures because they eat lots of insects. Some, however, also catch lizards, frogs, mice, or even birds. They only swallow liquid, so they paralyse their prey with venom and cover it with a thick substance. The innards of the captured prey turn into a kind of pulp which the spiders can drink. Some spiders are poisonous to humans, such as the one that lives in Brazil and loves to hide in houses in the middle of a pile of clothes or in shoes. It can leap 40 cm to attack an aggressor. Luckily, a serum to counteract its venom is available.

Do spiders have glue on their legs?

No, spiders can walk up walls and across ceilings because of suckers under their legs.

At the bottom of its hole, the trap-door spider waits for its prey. This spider can be over 15 cm long.

The Scorpion

The scorpion is not an insect. It is an arachnid, a member of the same family as the spider, and it lives in hot countries. It has two large pincers which it uses to capture its prey.

What a way to travel!
When they are born, baby scorpions travel everywhere on their mother's back. There may be any number of them, from 3 to 100, so they are often crammed together. They stay with their mother in this way until their first moult. After that, they have to leave their mother as quickly as possible, otherwise she will eat them!

When they mate, the male and female scorpion look as though they are dancing.

Do scorpions live in families?
No, they don't. Scorpions are solitary creatures who avoid each other. They only get together to mate. But this can end badly for the male, because afterwards he is often attacked and eaten by the female!

What else do scorpions eat?
They eat spiders and other soft-bodied creatures. They also eat small mice. A well fed scorpion can live for several months without food or water.

To defend itself, or to kill prey that struggles, the scorpion uses a poisonous sting at the end of its tail.

Index

A
Alligator 87
Anteaters
   Anteater, Giant . . 51
   Anteater, Spiny . . 55
Ants 112
Armadillo 53

B
Badger 26
Bat 10
Bears
   Brown Bear 29
   Koala Bear 58
   Polar Bear 30
Beaver 12
Bees 118-119
Bison 42
Blue Whale 67
Brown Bear 29
Butterflies . . . 120-121

C
Camel 48
Chameleon 90
Chamois 40
Cheetah 18
Chimpanzee 60
Crab 106-107
Crayfish 106-107
Crocodile 87
Crustaceans . . 106-107
Cuckoo 72

D
Dolphins 65
Dromedary 48
Duck-Billed
   Platypus 54

E
Eagle 78
Eel 97

Elephant 37
Elephant Seal 63

F
Flamingo 80
Fox 32
Frogs 94-95

G
Gazelle 41
Giant Anteater 51
Giant Panda 28
Giraffe 45

H
Hare 16
Hedgehog 8
Heron 81
Hippopotamus 38
Hyena 23

I
Insects 113-115

J
Jackal 33

K
Kangaroo 57
Killer Whale 66
Kiwi 82
Koala Bear 58
Komodo Dragon . . 92

L
Ladybird 111
Lemurs 59
Leopard 21
Lion 19
Lizards 91
Llama 49
Lobster 106
Lynx 22

M
Marmot 13
Marsupials 56
Meerkat 17
Mice 7
Mole 11
Molluscs 103-105
Monkeys 62
Moths 120-121
Musk Ox 43

O
Octopus 109
Okapi 46
Orang-Utan 61
Ostrich 83
Otter 24
Owls 71

P
Pangolin 52
Parrots 73
Peacock 86
Pelican 77
Penguin 76
Piranha 110
Polar Bear 30
Polecat 25
Porcupine 9
Possum 56
Prairie Dog 14
Puffin 75

R
Racoon 27
Rat 7
Rhinoceros 34

S
Salmon 98
Scorpion 124
Sea Anemone 108
Sea Horse 96
Sea Lions 64

Sea Turtle 93
Seagull 74
Seals 64
Shark 99
Shrew 6
Sloth 50
Slugs 105
Snails 105
Snakes 88-89
Spiders 122-123
Spiny Anteater 55
Squirrel 15
Stag 47
Starfish 102
Stork 85
Strange Fish . . 100-101
Swallow 68
Swan 84

T
Tapir 35
Termites 116
Tiger 20
Toads 94-95
Toucan 69
Turtle, Sea 93

V
Vulture 79

W
Walrus 63
Wasps 117
Water-Buffalo 44
Whales
   Blue Whale 67
   Killer Whale 66
Wild Boar 39
Wolf 31
Wombat 56
Woodpecker 70

Z
Zebra 36